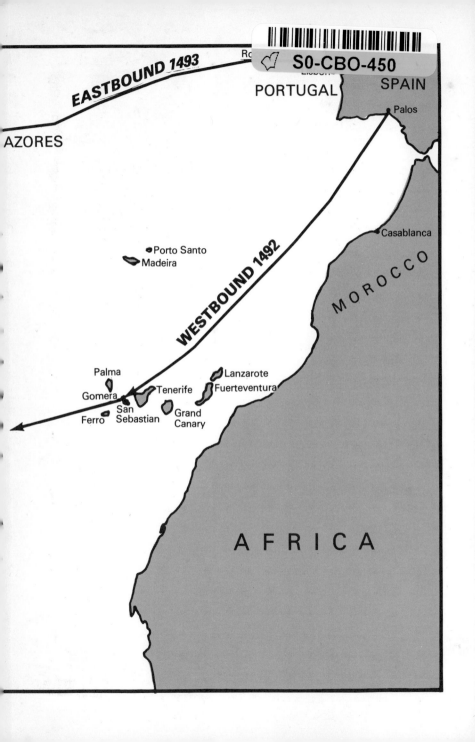

EASTBOUND 1493

AZORES

PORTUGAL

SPAIN

Palos

Porto Santo

Madeira

WESTBOUND 1492

Casablanca

MOROCCO

Palma

Lanzarote

Gomera

Tenerife

Fuerteventura

Ferro

San
Sebastian

Grand
Canary

AFRICA

COLUMBUS

EXPLORER FOR CHRIST

COLUMBUS

EXPLORER FOR CHRIST

by
Helen
Hinckley

HERALD PUBLISHING HOUSE
Drawer HH
Independence, Missouri

Library of Congress Cataloging in Publication Data

Jones, Helen Hinckley, 1903-
  Columbus, explorer for Christ.

  1. Colombo, Cristoforo. 2. Explorers-Italy—Biography.
3. America—Discovery and exploration—Spanish. I. Title.
E111.J7   970'.01'50924 [B]   76-30591
ISBN 0-8309-0169-8

Printed in the United States of America

I looked and beheld a man among the Gentiles, who was separated from the seed of my brethren [the American Indians] by the many waters; and I beheld the Spirit of God, that it came down and wrought upon the man; and he went forth upon the many waters, even to the seed of my brethren who were in the promised land.

—Book of Mormon, I Nephi 3:147.

From my first youth onward, I was a seaman and so continued until this day.... Wherever on the earth a ship has been, I have been.... The Lord was well disposed to my desire and He bestowed upon me courage and understanding; knowledge of seafaring He gave me in abundance, of astrology as much as was needed, and of geometry and astronomy likewise. Further he gave me joy and cunning in drawing maps and thereon cities and mountains, rivers, islands and harbors each one in its place. I have seen and truly I have studied all books...for which our Lord unlocked my mind, sent me upon the sea and gave me fire for the deed. Those who heard of my emprise called it foolish, mocked me and laughed. But who can doubt but that the Holy Ghost inspired me?

—Christopher Columbus

CHAPTER ONE

When the porter at the Monastery of Rábida heard the gate bell ring he got up slowly, easing his back with his hand. Taking one of the lighted candles from the table and holding it high he shuffled on slippered feet to open the gate. Who could be stopping at this hour? Someone begging for bread...or a blessing? When he opened the gate he looked up into the eyes of a tall white-haired stranger who held a small boy by the hand.

"Could I have a bit of bread and some water for the child? We have had a long walk from Palos."

"All is given in the name of Christ," the porter answered.

From beyond the dark hallway Friar Juan Pérez called, "The stranger is a foreigner. Bring him to me."

The man and child followed the porter through the narrow hall lighted only by the candle's glow. When they stood before Friar Juan Pérez the porter turned to look at the stranger. This was a young man, not more than thirty-five, not a grandfather as he had

9

first supposed. There were sand-colored strands in the white hair and a bridge of freckles across the nose.

"This is my son, Diego, Father," the stranger said. "I am Christopher—Christopher Columbus."

Juan Pérez gestured to the porter. "Give the child supper and a bed. These two shall not go forth tonight." Then he turned to his guest. "Christopher Columbus. I have heard the name."

"I am a navigator, and Palos is a seaport town. Perhaps you have heard of my adventures on the sea."

"Yes, that is it. There are many navigators here at Palos and in Seville. Have you heard of Martin Alonzo Pinzón? He and his brothers are navigators. They are celebrated for their expeditions."

"Yes, I have. And I am glad that you have heard of me."

The porter brought Columbus bread and cheese and wine.

"It is not often that a man of your distinction visits the Convent of Rábida," the Friar said. "Tell me about your adventures. What are your dreams? Where are you and the child going?"

"I hope to leave the child with you, Father, while I seek an audience with the royal sovereigns. I am going to offer my hopes and plans to Ferdinand and Isabella."

"Are you Spanish then? I imagined from your speech that you were Italian."

"I am originally from Genoa. Since an early age I have sailed the seas. My parents were wool carders, but I wanted nothing to do with their trade. I have sailed the Mediterranean Sea and have been as far west as the great Island of the North.* I have been an agent for many merchants, a navigator for many more. But when I was thirty-five I could feel my life going and I had done nothing for Christ or for myself. It was then I went to Portugal."

"Portugal is indeed the place for navigators," the friar said.

Both Columbus and Friar Juan Pérez knew about the great Portuguese prince, Henry the Navigator. It was Prince Henry who had thought it possible to reach India by sailing around Africa. Before Henry's time people had thought that a girdle of fire was always burning over the equator, that even the water boiled as it dashed against the white-hot coastal rocks. Henry had been with his father on an expedition into Africa against the Moors and knew that this was a myth. He gathered all of the scientists and scholars of his day to his retreat at Cape St. Vincent, and they assembled all that was known of geography and navigation into a system. Prince Henry had died before navigators had actually gone around Africa and east to the Indies, but he had left with them the obligation to find the eastern route.

"Eyes in Portugal are still turned to the route around Africa. King John II had no time to listen to me."

"But you stayed on?"

"Yes, I made maps and charts for other navigators. It was in Portugal that Diego was born."

The porter, having put Diego to bed, crept in and

*Iceland

11

sat on the floor, his back against the stone wall by the open fire.

Columbus told the friar how he had begun to feel more strongly every day that God wanted something special of him. He had gone to worship at the Convent of All Saints and there had met Dona Felipa, daughter of a cavalier who before his death had been Prince Henry's most famous navigator. Dona Felipa was interested in navigation. All her life she had heard of ships and sailing. She and Columbus were married.

"For a time we went to live with her mother."

Friar Juan Pérez nodded. "It is the usual thing when a mother is widowed," he said.

What was unusual, Columbus said, was that his mother-in-law became his teacher. She showed him her husband's maps and charts and told him of the Portuguese plans and ideas. But soon Columbus and Dona Felipa moved to an island which the family owned. Her sister, who lived on this island, was also married to a navigator. The two men talked frequently of the sea, the latest discoveries, the writings of the ancients, and the hallucinations of the people. Even some scholars thought that the Canaries and the Azores were bits left from the sinking island Atlantis which the ancients believed had once been the seat of all learning and culture. People who lived on these islands thought that they saw land still farther to the west covered with high mountains.

"I know that the world is round," Columbus told his brother-in-law. "I know that you can reach the East by traveling west."

"Why don't you write to Paola Toscanelli about your

12 Paola Toseanelli - a Italian mathematician astronomer, and cosmographer

plans? Although he is Italian his learning might carry great weight with King John," his brother-in-law suggested.

So Columbus had written, and Toscanelli's answer had been encouraging.

"So you took the idea to King John?" Friar Juan Pérez asked.

"After innumerable delays I took the idea to King John," Columbus answered.

The story was a long one. The porter dozed by the fire and the friar leaned forward, resting his chin on his hand.

"I think it was the invention of the astrolabe that caused King John to summon me at last."

John II had become king of Portugal in 1481. He carried on his grand uncle's enthusiasm for exploration and scientific study. It was his scientists that discovered the astrolabe. With it a seaman, by noting the height of the sun from the horizon, could determine his distance from the equator. Now the mariner could trace his course by both the compass and the astrolabe.

When Columbus was summoned, he proposed that the king furnish him with ships and men that he might undertake to find an even shorter way to India than around Africa. John listened, then consulted his scientists. They suggested to the king that another navigator, perhaps using Columbus's maps and charts, could sail secretly and test Columbus's theory.

While Columbus waited to hear from King John, his wife died. When the secret ship came back and reported that there was nothing except waves and storms to the west Columbus felt betrayed by the

astrolabe —

13

king he had trusted. Without his wife or faith in his king, what was left in Portugal for him? John offered him another audience, but he refused it. He had come to Spain, bringing his little son with him.

"Here I hope to find assistance," Columbus told the friar. "But it is not easy to arrange an audience with the royal sovereigns."

The friar shook his head. "Now it is most difficult. Queen Isabella and King Ferdinand are determined to defeat the Moors, and battles with the Moors are costly. They wish to expel the Jews, and that is a tremendous undertaking. They are putting every effort into making all Spain a Christian nation."

"Yet my dreams are much greater. On the other side of the world there are millions of souls waiting to be brought to Christ. I . . . "

"And one must go west to reach the east. This is what scientists say, but I don't understand it. Nevertheless you must rest here for a while. I have scientific friends who can understand all of your plans. Very soon Fray Antonio de Marchena will be at our priory. He is in high repute as an astronomer. He will understand all that you have to say, and he has friends in high places." The friar shook his head slowly. "There is so little that I understand of all that you have told me."

"But there is something about my plans that you can understand better than any other," Columbus said. He moved closer to the friar and dropped his voice so that only the two could hear. "In India there are many people who have never heard of Christ Jesus. I feel that for the glory of God I must seek them out. Christ must be taught to 'every kindred, tongue, and people.'" His voice dropped still lower and he glanced at the porter dozing by the fire. Almost in a whisper he said. "This is my mission. Christ expects it of me, and I am in the hollow of God's hand!"

CHAPTER TWO

Almost at once five-year-old Diego fitted into the quiet life of Rábida. There was time for play with the other children for whom the good fathers were caring. There was time for lessons, and Diego was a bright and curious child. Once he went on tiptoe into the room where Columbus was studying. "Father, have you no time for me?" he asked timidly.

Columbus took the child on his knee and ran his hand over the boy's hair. "Aren't you happy here?"

"But, Father . . ."

"I know," Columbus said. "I know that you miss your mother and that I am a navigator with a dream, while you are a small boy. Things will be different when I have seen the royal sovereigns."

Columbus turned back to the maps and charts that he would show Fray Antonio when the Custodio arrived at the priory. His head throbbed with the excitement. The Custodio was a church man but also an astronomer. He would understand both Columbus's plans and his feeling that he was "in the hand of God."

Priory - a small monastery

When Fray Antonio arrived Columbus could scarcely wait for him to be welcomed at the priory before he spread his maps on the wooden table before him and began his explanation. "There is no use in taking time to prove to you that the earth is round. That is the way I would have to begin with most churchmen. But you are an astronomer and you accept that idea already."

"Yes," Fray Antonio said. "But there are other questions. What is on the other side of the round earth? How wide are the seas? How far is it from the Canary Islands to the islands off the shores of India?"

"The seas are narrow. I am sure of that. Have not seamen picked up pieces of wood from trees that never grew in Europe or Africa that must have been brought by the ocean from across the water?" In his books by Pliny, Ptolemy, Pierre D'Ailly, and Sylvius, Columbus had underlined the parts that seemed to support his ideas and written long annotations in the margins. Now he opened these books.

Fray Antonio drew his chair closer to the table to read the underlined sections. He was familiar with the books and recognized that some of the best scholars agreed with Columbus that the ocean was narrow. A mariner could reach the Indies with ease if he resupplied at the Canaries.

"But little good it does you for me to believe you and share your enthusiasm," Fray Antonio said. "True, I am Custodio of the Franciscan subprovince of Seville, but ships and money—they are strangers to me!"

17

"Forgive me," Columbus said. "I counted too much on this conversation. But it is encouraging to know that I can express my ideas in Spanish well enough to be understood."

"You not only share your ideas, you share your enthusiasm," Fray Antonio said. "Now who is intelligent and rich?"

Columbus sat with his hands clenching the table. "There must be someone."

"There is someone," Fray Antonio almost shouted. "Why didn't I think of him before? There is Don Enrique de Guzmán, Duke of Medina Sidonia. He is the wealthiest subject of our sovereigns. Apply to him. I will introduce you. I hope he will listen and believe."

It did not take Columbus long to make application to the duke, and when he received an invitation to come at once he rolled up his maps and prepared to set out for Medina Sidonia.

Diego followed his father to the gate of the priory. There were tears in his eyes, and his hands were clenched into fists. "Good-bye, Father," he said. "May God keep you."

Columbus knelt to kiss him. "And may God keep you, and give you a father who is Admiral of the Ocean Seas," he said.

There was no long wait in Seville. Don Enrique had received Fray Antonio's letter and was anxious to see Columbus. He made him comfortable in his home as an honored guest and then bent over the maps and charts. Columbus was an excellent map maker, and Don Enrique was impressed with what he saw. "Of course the world is round. What intelligent man would not believe that? But of its size we have no idea. How wide is the ocean?"

So again Columbus opened his books. He believed the ocean was narrow and a journey to the Indies not much farther than one he had already taken to the Islands of the North.

He turned in one of his books to a chapter he had underlined and annotated. This chapter in *Imago Mundi*, the most comprehensive world geography of the time, described the mighty rivers, the gold, the silver, the precious jewels. Columbus skipped over the sections about the elephants, the parrots, the griffins, the monsters. Don Enrique would be much more impressed with the account of islands where pearls were as easily picked up as pebbles.

The two heads were together as they read the Latin text. Wonderful!

It did not take Don Enrique long to make a decision. "I'll do it! How many caravels will be needed? How many men? What supplies? When is the best time for such an expedition to sail?"

After all the waiting on King John of Portugal, after the negotiations with Italian bankers, after disappointment followed by more disappointment, Columbus thought God must surely be working with him now.

"It will take me some time to find answers to all of your questions, but there *are* answers," Columbus promised. "My brother Bartholomew is in France. Perhaps he will join me and add his practical knowledge to mine. Together we'll work out every detail."

"Excellent," Don Enrique said. And this is the way they left it.

Columbus had seldom felt happier—nearer the successful pursuit of his whole dream—than he did now. Surely God was with him. His good fortune had begun when he had seen the weathered buildings of the Convent of Rábida on a bluff overlooking the port of Palos. Such establishments often cared for children, he had thought, and together he and little Diego had walked the dusty road to the priory. There he had met Friar Juan Pérez who had invited him to stay to talk with Fray Antonio de Marchena. Fray Antonio had been impressed and had given him an introduction to Don Enrique de Guzmán who had been caught in the fire of Columbus's enthusiasm. Now the expedition was in Columbus's hands—and in God's.

Just when his dream seemed to be coming true Don Enrique had a foolish political quarrel, and the royal sovereigns ordered him to leave Seville. The negotiations ended. Don Enrique would never be able to furnish the ships and men for the expedition.

Deeply discouraged, Columbus rolled up his maps and charts and packed his precious books. "Why not try Don Luis de la Cerda, Count of Medina Celi?" Don Enrique had suggested before he left Seville. "He is not a man of enormous wealth but he does own a large merchant fleet and a sizable establishment at Puerta Santa Maria."

Columbus couldn't be discouraged for long. His were

more than a man's plans. Deep in his consciousness he felt that he was bound on a mission for Christ. Work and prayer would lift his depression. He would go at once to the Count.

Stopping by Rábida, he visited Diego and Friar Juan Pérez. Then he went on to Puerta Santa Maria where he would fan the flame of enthusiasm that had burned so high during his visit with Don Enrique.

But the Duke of Medina Celi was not like Don Enrique. He did not make up his mind at once. He made Columbus a guest in his house while he studied the maps and charts and talked to his navigators and pilots. He was not the sort of man to say, "I'll do it. How many ships will you need?" Carefully he considered every part of Columbus's plan: the ships, the men, the supplies, the material that would be needed to trade with the Indians when Columbus landed in India. He was two years in reaching his conclusions. Then he said, "This is too great an undertaking for a citizen. It would better fit our royal sovereigns. If Isabella approves, I'll undertake it."

"And if not?" Columbus asked.

"It is a sound plan. I think she will approve," was the Duke of Medina Celi's answer.

CHAPTER THREE

When Queen Isabella received the letter from the Duke of Medina Celi she didn't say yes or no to his appeal. Instead she sent a summons to Columbus to appear at court and present his plan to her. If he would come to Cordova at once she would give him an audience. If her decision was favorable, the Duke of Medina Celi could outfit the three or four caravels that Columbus needed and he could sail with her blessings.

On January 20, 1486, Columbus arrived in Cordova. The king and queen had already left for Madrid. He would have to wait until their return.

With little to do while he waited, Columbus dropped into an apothecary shop near the Port of Cordova. The owner was an Italian like Columbus. The shop was the informal meeting place for surgeons, physicians, scientists. At the apothecary shop he started a conversation with young Diego de Harana who was deeply interested in navigation and listened with wide-eyed excitement to Columbus's story of his many voyages.

One day Diego de Harana invited Columbus to his father's house. Although his father was a wine presser—not an elegant trade—he was a man of culture and wide interests. Columbus fitted into the household at once. There he met Diego's orphaned cousin, Beatriz. He was attracted to her and may have thought of marrying her. Columbus's first wife, little Diego's mother, had been an aristocrat, and his marriage to her had been helpful in his career. Too, she had been his first love. He did not marry Beatriz, but they became more than friends.

In April the royal sovereigns returned to Cordova. In May Columbus was summoned before them.

Columbus had seen much of the world. He had had an audience with King John II of Portugal. Never had he seen such luxury as he saw in the audience chamber of the Alcazar of Cordova. The queen—almost the same age as Columbus—was tall, commanding, and beautiful. Her features were perfect; her skin was fair and smooth; her eyes were deep blue, and her hair resembled shining copper. Beside her King Ferdinand looked ill tempered and plain. But Columbus knew that the king was a genius at diplomacy. His kingdoms, bordering on the Mediterranean, had strong maritime traditions, but they looked toward the East, not toward the West. Columbus's hope for approval lay with Isabella. Perhaps she would give her blessing to his proposed project at once.

He was ardent in his presentation of his plan. "I felt kindled as with a fire from high," he later wrote in his diary. He knew that his royal sovereigns had united León, Castile, and Aragon just twelve years before. Isabella was such an ardent Christian that she felt the entire kingdom should be united under Christ. The royal sovereigns were battling the Moslem moors and expelling or converting the Jews. Especially for Isabella's ears he told of his deep conviction that God wanted him to carry the message of Christ to the uncounted infidels in India.

Tactfully Isabella answered that there were certain practical questions that must be answered. Did her counselors who were expert in such matters think that the journey he proposed was practicable? Could the crown afford to pay for such an expedition while the royal sovereigns were engaged in fighting the Moors? She would organize the commission under Fray Hernando de Talavera to examine the project.

Columbus didn't feel discouraged when he left the audience chamber. Not only had the queen been interested and gracious but she had put him in the temporary care of the comptroller of finances and arranged for him to meet the Archbishop of Toledo, the Grand Cardinal of Spain. God was certainly smiling on him, he thought, though things would certainly have been simpler if the queen had merely given the Duke of Medina Celi her blessings.

With enthusiasm he began to prepare his submission for the Talavera Commission.

The meetings of the commission dragged on. Almost from the first Columbus felt that the commissioners were unfriendly. When the Court went to Salamanca for Christmas the commission and Columbus went, too. In Salamanca he made a friend, Dominican Father

Diego de Deza, who later was archbishop of Seville. He believed that Columbus's plans were both practicable and desirable. The support of Diego de Deza made it possible for him to endure the silly questions and foolish jests of members of ´ the commission. These men didn't know enough even to ask questions, he told Diego de Deza.

At last the commission reached a decision, but Talavera didn't announce it. The queen put Columbus on a small pension—about the size of the salary of an able seaman.

The Talavera Commission made no announcement.

The pension was discontinued.

Still there was no announcement.

Malaga, the last Moorish seaport, fell.

The Talavera Commission remained silent.

Columbus spent his time making and selling maps and charts. He studied and added to the underlining and notes in his four special books. Every day he expected a summons from the queen.

Perhaps the brightest event in these difficult years was the birth of his second son, Ferdinand, to Beatriz.

It wasn't until 1489 that Talavera was ready to issue his report. All local and municipal officials were ordered to give Columbus food and shelter as he traveled to join the royal sovereigns at their camp outside of Baza, a Moorish city which was under seige.

Now Talavera was ready to issue the commission's report. Columbus had felt that members of the commission hadn't listened and didn't understand even when they heard, but the sovereigns summoning him to the camp raised his hopes.

"The commission judges the promises and offers of Columbus to be impossible and vain and worthy of rejection."

Columbus was bitterly disappointed. Worse than the recommendation for rejection were the reasons given for the negative report:

1. A voyage to the Indies would take three years.

2. The Western Ocean is infinite and perhaps unnavigable.

3. If he reaches the Antipodes [the land on the other side of the earth from Europe] he cannot get back. How can a ship sail uphill?

4. On the other hand there are probably no Antipodes because the greater part of the globe is coverd with water. Augustine says so.

5. Of the five zones only three are habitable.

6. So many centuries after the creation it is unlikely that anyone could find hitherto unknown lands of value.

There was no appeal from the commission's report. Isabella did say that the royal sovereigns had neither accepted nor rejected the report and that Columbus could bring the matter to their attention again after Granada had been conquered by their armies.

Again Columbus waited. For almost nine months he stayed in Seville. Then totally disgusted he returned to Rábida.

Six years had passed since he had first seen the Convent of Rábida on the bluff overlooking the ocean and had determined to leave his small son there. Six years and he was no better off, no nearer to the goal that he felt God had set for him.

The same old porter, grown feebler and slower,

answered the door and ushered him into Fray Juan Pérez's study. "I am disgusted with Seville," he told the friar. "Even the children in Seville put their fingers to their heads and mock me. God cannot expect me to endure more."

CHAPTER FOUR

Friar Juan Pérez had never seen Columbus so discouraged. He sat with his elbows on the table, his head in his hands. When the friar sent for Diego, Columbus looked up. "You must leave Rábida now," Columbus told the boy. "We are through with Spain. We will go to France."

"Why France?" Friar Juan Pérez wanted to know.

"My brother Bartholomew who is well versed in my proposals is in France. He will make an arrangement for an audience with the king."

"Surely there is hope in Spain," the friar protested.

After Diego had left them Columbus told Friar Juan Pérez the long story. He told him of the Duke of Medina Celi and his offer to outfit three or four caravels if only Isabella would approve of the project, of his audience with the queen, of his appearance before the Talavera Commission, and of the endless wait before Talavera issued his negative report.

"And what does Queen Isabella say now?"

Columbus shrugged his shoulders. "She says to approach the royal sovereigns with the plans when the Moors are entirely defeated."

"Why not wait for that time, then?" the friar asked.

"Wait, wait, wait! I am going to be an old man with waiting."

"This much I ask of you," the friar insisted. "I will bring the learned men and experienced navigators of Palos to hear you and look at your charts. You must see if they agree with the Talavera Commission."

"I must go to France," Columbus insisted. "What difference will it make if the learned men do not agree with the commission?"

Juan Pérez put one blue-veined hand on Columbus's shoulder. "If the practical men of Palos agree that your plans are workable I myself will go to the queen."

"You, Father?" Columbus asked.

"I was once confessor to the queen. She will see me."

So Columbus waited to see the learned men and the practical navigators of Palos.

Dr. Fernandez, a physician, was the best authority in Palos on astronomy and cosmography. He thought Columbus's maps and charts were excellent. He had long thought that the earth was round and that sailing west would bring one to the East. Martin Alonzo Pinzón, a leading shipowner of Palos, was more interested in what could be expected in the way of gain when the Indies were reached.

Columbus responded to their interest with new enthusiasm. When these two learned men and others from Palos said that the Commission of Talavera had not been wise in its report, Fray Pérez was delighted. He remembered Columbus's solemn words to him the first night he had been in Rábida. "This is my mission. Christ expects it of me, and I am in God's hand."

The queen was in the new, fortified city of Santa Fe which had been built to serve as the Castilian headquarters for the seige of Granada. A pilot named Sebastian Rodriguez carried the friar's personal letter to the queen. It took just two weeks for Friar Juan Pérez to receive a reply. Juan Perez must come to Santa Fe at once, and Columbus was to wait at Rábida for a summons of his own.

How would Juan Perez make the trip to Santa Fe? He was far too old to go by foot. With money given him by Martin Alonzo Pinzón, Columbus rented a mule to carry the old friar to visit the queen.

It wasn't long before Columbus received a letter summoning him to the queen's court. With the letter came a gift of money to buy some handsome clothes and to charter a mule. Late in August 1491 Columbus appeared before the queen. If she said yes, he would plunge into preparations for the long planned voyage. If she said no he would leave for France.

She said neither yes nor no. Again she put the whole enterprise into the hands of a committee of astrologers, pilots, and mariners. They thought the plans workable and passed them on to the Royal Council.

Columbus, who once would have been satisfied with three or four small ships, now asked for honors, titles, and a share of any wealth discovered by the expedition. Where now was the feeling that Christ had called him on a mission to carry Christianity to "nations now in darkness"?

30

Granada fell in January 1492. Columbus marched in the procession that entered the last stronghold of the Moslems in Catholic Spain. As soon as the celebration was over he was called before the royal sovereigns. The answers to his plea—the outcome of six years of presenting his plans and waiting—was a final no. He had asked too much.

Angered at having waited six and a half years, Columbus saddled his mule, packed his precious books and maps in the saddlebags, and with Friar Juan set out for Cordova. Perhaps the money that was left from the queen's gift would take him to France. If not he had made maps and charts before. He was still an excellent navigator. But he resented all that wasted time!

They had gone only ten miles when they were over-taken by a messenger from the queen. She commanded that they return to the court at once. Obediently they retraced their steps.

They did not know that Luis de Santangel, an influen-tial man and a friend of Columbus had gone at once to the queen and told her that she was missing the opportunity of the century. There was so little money needed and so much to be gained. He had been so persuasive that Queen Isabella had offered to pledge her jewels, though Santangel, who was keeper of the purse, said that would not be necessary.

Columbus stood before the queen once more. This time there was no committee. The answer was yes. The purchase and outfitting of the ships would come to about 2,000,000 maravedis ($14,000). The salaries of the men would amount to 150,000 maravedis each month. The royal sovereigns would raise a part of the necessary money, Luis Santangel would raise some, and Columbus would borrow 200,000 from such friends as Medina Celi.

As soon as the lawyers had finished their haggling about commissions, titles, and the sharing of treasure, the great voyage could begin and Columbus would indeed be Admiral of the Ocean Seas.

On May 12, 1492, Columbus left Granada for Palos, from which he would sail on his remarkable voyage of discovery.

CHAPTER FIVE

All of the men and boys in Palos were jostling each other in the square before the Church of St. George. The mayor was there, and so were his councilors. Francisco Fernandez, the notary public, held in his hand a letter that Columbus had brought from the royal sovereigns.

When he unrolled the parchment the men stood silent. "Ferdinand and Isabella, by the Grace of God, King and Queen of Castille, Leon, Aragon, Sicily, etc. to you, Diego Rodriguez Prieto, and all the inhabitants of the town of Palos, greeting and grace."

But the big news was still to come. Palos was ordered to furnish two caravels to Columbus within ten days. Two ships to sail into unknown waters! To the seamen of Palos that was unthinkable. Perhaps Columbus thought that the people would be enthusiastic. The foreigner could think again. In their letter the royal sovereigns had said that seamen would be paid from the royal treasury four months in advance, but what would four months' pay mean if a man might be gone forever?

Why Palos? Why not Seville? Why not Cadiz? These, the bigger ports in Andalusia, were crowded with refugees seeking an opportunity to depart Christian Spain. Just a month before Isabella and Ferdinand had said yes to Columbus's request they had issued an edict giving the Jews who had lived in Spain for centuries and contributed so much to her business and intellectual life just four months either to become Catholics or leave the country. As Columbus returned from Granada to Palos he found the roads clogged with men, women, and children, carrying their possessions or walking beside overloaded donkey carts. Now Isabella had said that every Jew-bearing ship must leave port on August 2, 1492. Cadiz would be far too crowded, seamen too busy in the larger ports. Besides, for some little breaking of an unimportant rule the royal sovereigns had fined the town of Palos the use of two ships for a year.

It took ten weeks, not ten days, for Palos to furnish the *Niña* and *Pinta* and for Columbus to charter the *Santa María* and furnish the three vessels with supplies and firewood.

The *Pinta* and *Niña* were caravels, small light vessels that could fly before the wind. The *Santa María* was slightly larger. Even though it was the flagship, it was not the favorite of Columbus. He liked the *Niña* best.

Having procured the vessels he then had to find crews. No one wanted to sign for the journey. The unemployed seamen who hung around the plaza didn't say that they were frightened; they merely said that nothing would be gained by the voyage. The Portuguese had tried it, they told each other, and what had they found? Besides, Columbus was a stranger who happened to be in good with Isabella and Ferdinand, and who could trust a stranger? But when Martin Alonzo Pinzón, the leading mariner in the town, signed on to command the *Pinta* and Juan Niño signed as master of the *Niña*, seamen began to change their minds. There must be something good in this voyage, they thought, if such well known mariners were eager to go.

At last all was ready. The water flasks were filled at a fountain near the Church of St. George, and every man and boy confessed his sins, received absolution, and partook of Communion.

Columbus knelt in confession. Now, at long last, this enterprise which he felt was in God's hands was about to be launched. Diego, his son, was at the Royal Court, the companion of Isabella and Ferdinand's son, the prince. Everything was right in Christopher Columbus's world. In his sea journal he wrote that he was setting out to "discover the nature and disposition of them all [the people of the Antipodes] and the means to be taken for the conversion of them to our holy faith."

Counting on favorable winds he planned to sail first to the Canaries, then straight west to the Indies.

Early Friday morning, August 3, Columbus went to the Church of St. George and took Communion. Before dawn he was aboard his flagship, and "in the name of Jesus" gave command to get under way. Carried by the outgoing tide, the three vessels silently dropped down the river. As they passed La Rábida the friars were chanting their liturgical hymn. Columbus removed his hat. The seamen dropped to their knees. The hymn seemed to bless the tiny armada that was going out to carry Christ to every "nation, kindred, tongue, and people."

At eight in the morning the three vessels crossed the bar. In six days, on August 9, they sighted the Canaries, ordinarily an eight-day voyage, even though the *Pinta's* rudder had worked loose and had to be temporarily repaired at sea.

On the evening of August 12 Columbus anchored in San Sebastian, Gomera. Here he put in water, beef jerky, firewood, and other supplies, then sailed for Las Palmas where he was to meet the other two vessels.

Martin Alonzo Pinzón was supervising the local blacksmiths in remaking the *Pinta's* rudder. Columbus had the *Niña's* triangular sails changed to square rigging. The triangular sails gave greater speed, but the square rigging was better for difficult ocean voyages.

Early morning of September 9 Columbus went to the Church of the Assumption. He heard mass and renewed his covenants with Christ to carry His message to the infidel.

Anchor was weighed for the last time in the known world. Every man who had signed on at Palos was on board. None had deserted. By September 9 even Tenerife, the 12,000-foot volcano belching flames and smoke, was out of sight.

Before them lay the ocean.

CHAPTER SIX

Columbus watched the sails of the *Santa Maria* fill with the west-blowing trade winds. From the ship the ocean looked like a great round plate of deep gray water, ever changing yet ever the same. He had never felt more joyous. Three times a day he went to his cabin to pray. Never during all the time he had sought help for his expedition had he felt more strongly that God was watching over him.

The men prayed, too, perhaps because they were alone on an uncharted ocean, perhaps because prayer was a usual part of ship life. They did not go to their cabins to pray in secret because they had no cabins. The common seamen didn't even have individual bunks. When their watch was over they propped themselves against a convenient support, so they wouldn't roll with the movement of the ship, and slept. Each half hour the grummet—the ship's boy—turned the hour glass so that the sand running down could tell them of the passing of time. If the grummet was the youngest one on board he also conducted the prayers. Columbus, as well as the others, believed that God listened more readily to the prayers of the innocent than to the prayers of men who had lived long enough to sin. Besides working and praying and sleeping and eating, the men amused themselves with their sea chanties. This trip with Columbus was turning out to be a great adventure. "The weather was like April in Andalusia, the only thing wanting was to hear the nightingale."

How wide was the ocean? Columbus had insisted that it was narrow and could be crossed in a few days. Now he wasn't so sure. Perhaps the men would grow alarmed if his maps and charts, none drawn from experience, proved wrong. He began to take a private reckoning of the distance covered each day, and a public reckoning that showed a shorter distance for his crew.

The voyage had begun on September 9. The first few days went by like a dream. But Columbus's peace of mind was broken on September 13 when his compass, pointing due north, didn't point exactly to the north star. He told the mariners that the star revolved around a pole. He did not know, then, how right his explanation was. All astronomers believed that the star was stationary. He was only glad when the needle once again pointed to the star.

On September 14 the men saw birds, "red-tails" and terns. Columbus could not imagine birds that needed no land to rest on during their long flights southward. Not knowing the habits of seabirds, he thought their presence meant that land was near. He didn't know that the Azores, 570 miles behind them, was the nearest land.

On September 16 they saw green seaweed, and on September 17 they plucked a tiny live crab out of the weeds. By September 21 they were sailing through a green meadow of seaweed. Surely land would be sighted at any moment.

Since September 18 the three ships had not made good time. The west-blowing winds had died down. Columbus did not realize that he had left the trade winds. On September 22 he told the men that he was glad to see the variable winds. Many had asked how the ships would ever sail back to Spain if the winds blew always in one direction. And on September 23, when the seas were high, instead of being discouraged Columbus wrote, "Thus very useful to me was the high seas, a sign such as had not appeared since in the time of the Jews when they came up out of Egypt and grumbled against Moses who delivered them out of captivity."

Never once did Columbus lose confidence in God. Frequently he recalled Psalm 107: "They that go down to the sea in ships and occupy their business in great waters; these men see the works of the Lord, and his wonders of the deep. For at his word the stormy winds ariseth, which lifteth up the winds thereof."

On September 25, at sunset, Martin Alonzo Pinzón shouted, "Land, land!" There was a great scurrying, and everyone who could swarmed up the rigging. All declared they saw land and that evening they chanted "Gloria in excelsis Deo." But in the morning there was no land in sight. Clouds on the horizon had deceived everybody.

Now the grumbling, of which Columbus had been

aware since September 18, began to grow louder. By October 1 looks had grown sullen, and he noticed the men glancing at him from under lowered brows. Not that he blamed them. They had now been twenty-one days without sight of land. "A few days to cross the unchartered sea," he had promised. If he had been wrong about the width of the sea he might be wrong about everything. Perhaps there was no land at all.

The ships were traveling faster now, but the mutinous talk had grown to violent gestures. Columbus told the more violent men that if they wished they could kill him and those who agreed with him, but they could never again go back to Spain and live.

On October 4 a flock of petrels raised new hope of land and on October 7, the *Niña*, running ahead, fired a gun to announce landfall. But this was another mistake. An award of 10,000 maravedis had been announced for the first man who sighted land. Now Columbus said that anyone who gave a false announcement would forfeit the prize even though he later earned it.

In the midst of the growing mutiny Columbus kept the ships moving westward. When he saw a flight of migrating birds he changed his course slightly to follow the "feathered pilots."

On October 9 the seas were calm and rapid travel was impossible. The three ships drew together, and the captain came aboard the *Santa María* where the men were most restless.

On Wednesday, October 10, this discontent flared into open mutiny. The men felt that they had done more than enough to bring Columbus's mad dream to reality.

A few days? Over a month had passed since they had last seen land. What had been the promises when they had sighted seabirds and meadows of seaweed? Promises. . . nothing but promises! The Basques and Galicians that made up the crew of the *Santa María* saw Columbus as a foreigner, not one of their own. They insisted that the ships turn back.

Columbus felt that, called of God, he must move forward. But he understood the men and knew that there was justice in their complaints and demands. He had been mistaken about the narrow ocean. The men were well aware of that. He knew that they could not feel his conviction that he was in God's hands. He talked to them and told them what wonderful advantages they would have when the voyage was successfully completed. Now the wind was from the east and the sea was high. There was no turning back today, at least. He asked for three more days— just three more days!

Grumbling, the men agreed. On Thursday, October 11, the wind filled the sails, and the ships charged along.

And then there were true signs of land. *Niña* crewmen picked up a branch with a flower on it such as never grew in the sea. Those on the *Pinta* found a piece of board, a land plant, and a carved stick. Perhaps three days would be long enough.

At sunset, after prayers, Columbus spoke to the men of the *Santa María*. "Our Lord has been good to us. He has cared for us and given us good weather and good winds." He then asked the nightwatch to keep a "clear eye" for land breakers since the ships, taking advantage of the wind, would sail all night. What fortunate man would wear a new silk doublet and receive the 10,000 maravedis for first sighting land?

The direction was changed from north of west to west, and the ships moved faster than they had during the entire voyage.

At 11:00 p.m. Columbus, standing on the stern castle, thought he saw a moving light. He called Pedro Gutierrez, who saw it too. When a seaman sang out "Lumbre tierra," Columbus's page boy said, "My master has already seen it."

It was 2:00 a.m., October 12, when Rodrego de Triana on the *Niña* saw a white cliff, and then another, then a stretch of land connecting the cliffs. "Tierra, tierra!" he shouted. Martin Alonzo checked, and he saw it too. He fired the gun, already loaded, and waited for the flagship.

It wasn't safe to approach the land more closely because there might be reefs and shoals that could not be seen in the darkness. The three ships of the little armada—the *Niña*, *Pinta*, and *Santa María*—waited until morning before the men could reach the land and kiss the soil.

The most important voyage in all history was over.

CHAPTER SEVEN

At daybreak the voyagers sighted naked people on the beach. Columbus, Martin Alonzo Pinzón, and Vincent Yáñez, his brother, went ashore in the ship's boat. Columbus carried the royal standard, and the Pinzóns carried banners of the expedition. They all knelt on the ground and "embraced it with tears of joy for the immeasurable mercy of having reached it." Then Columbus arose and gave the island the name of San Salvador. The curious Indians and the Spaniards who had come from the ship gathered around him. He had earned the title of admiral. The men who had doubted that the ships would ever reach land begged his pardon for their fears. Columbus then reached toward the natives. Later, in his log he wrote:

In order that we might win good friendship, because I knew that they were people who could better be freed and converted to our Holy Faith by love than by force, I gave to some of them red caps and to some glass beads, which they hung on their necks, and many other things of slight value, in which they took much pleasure; they remained so much our friends that it was a marvel; and later they came swimming to the ships' boats in which we were, and brought us parrots and cotton thread in skeins and many other things, and we swapped them for other things that we gave them, such as little glass beads and hawks' bells. Finally they swapped and gave everything they had, with good will, but it appeared to us that these people were very poor in everything. They go quite naked as their mothers bore them; and also the women, although I didn't see more than one really young girl. All that I saw were young men, none of them more than thirty years old, very well made, of very handsome bodies and very good faces.... They bear no arms nor know thereof; for I showed them swords and they grasped them by the blade and cut themselves through ignorance; they have no iron. Their darts are a kind of rod without iron, and some have at the end a fish's tooth and others other things. They are generally fairly tall and good looking. I saw some who had marks of wounds on their bodies, and made signs to ask them what it was, and they showed how people of other islands which are near came there and wished to capture them and they defended themselves. And I believed and now believe that people do come here from the mainland to take them as slaves. They ought to be good servants and of good skill, for I see that they repeat very quickly all that is said to them, and I believe that they would easily be made Christians, because it seemed to me that they belonged to no religion. I, please our Lord, will carry off six of them at my departure to your Highnesses, so that they may learn to speak.

But what strange people they were! Why weren't they black of skin and kinky of hair since they lived on the same latitude as the Africans? Or perhaps the latitude was the same as the Canaries. These handsome young men were no darker than the men of the Canaries, but they certainly were different.

On October 13 many of the young men came to the ships in canoes hollowed out from great logs to see the Spaniards and to trade with them.

Columbus had brought a man, skilled in Arabic, to

44

be an interpreter. He thought that the Arabic language was the root of all languages and anyone who knew it could understand anything. But this interpreter was of no use with these natives. Only sign language was useful. Columbus thought that the men who came out in their canoes were saying to each other, "Come and see the men who came from heaven. Bring them food and drink." At least the natives threw themselves on their faces, pointed toward heaven, and brought food and drink.

Columbus and his companions were delirious with joy. Yet Columbus was amazed, too. Marco Polo, writing of Cipangu (Japan) had described a palace roofed with gold, golden pavements, and pearls in abundance. San Salvador must be an outer island, and he must press on and find the greater island. The sure sign of Marco Polo's India was gold.

October 14 the armada left San Salvador to search for Cipangu. Columbus had decided that an island called Colba (Cuba) must be the fabled island. His unwilling Indian guides had seemed to inform him that Cuba was where gold could be found.

Columbus found other islands, but no gold. There were naked savages willing to trade excellent cotton for falcon's bells and glass beads. There were the most beautiful trees he had ever seen. There were singing birds and sweet smelling plants. Columbus saw for the first time parasite plants on the trees and described in his diary trees with "branches of different kinds, all on one tree, and one twig of one kind and another of another, and so unlike it is the greatest wonder of the world."

45

He named the islands he discovered Santa María de la Concepcion, Fernandino, and Isabela.

Everywhere Columbus went he was impressed with the natives. In his desire to find gold he didn't forget his primary purpose—to bring new souls to Christ. He wrote:

I have observed that these people have no religion, neither are they idolators, but are a very gentle race, without the knowledge of iniquity, they neither kill nor steal nor carry weapons and are so timid that one of our men might put a hundred of them to flight, although they will readily sport and play tricks with them. They have a knowledge that there is a God above, and are firmly persuaded that we come from heaven. They very quickly learn such prayers as we repeat to them, and also make the sign of the cross. Your Highnesses, therefore, should adopt the resolution of converting them to Christianity, in which enterprise I am of opinion that a very short space of time would suffice to gain to our holy faith multitudes of people. . . .

But he had neither the language nor the time to begin the work himself.

I have no doubt most serene Princes that were proper devout and religious persons to come among them and learn their language, it would be an easy matter to convert them all to Christianity, and I hope in our Lord that your Highnesses will devote yourselves with much diligence to this object and bring into the Church so many multitudes, inasmuch as you have exterminated those who refused to confess the Father, Son, and Holy Ghost, so that having ended your days (as we are all mortal) you may leave your dominions in a tranquil condition, free from heresy and wickedness, and meet with a favourable reception before the eternal creator, whom it may please to grant you a long life and great increase of kingdoms and dominions, with the will and disposition to promote, as you always have done, the holy Christian religion. Amen.

The Spaniards were amazed to see the natives

with smoke coming out of their mouths. The Indians wrapped a tobacco leaf around other leaves, making a primitive cigar. To light them the adults were often accompanied by boys who carried firebrands.

The crewmen enjoyed poking around in the native houses, though Columbus wanted to keep the Indians' friendship and warned his men not to touch a thing even when the owners were absent. It was on one of these uninvited visits that the men first saw the hamacus (hammock) which was later to make so much difference in the life of the seamen.

Sunday, October 28, the three ships anchored in the mouth of a river so impressive that Columbus's friend La Casas wrote:

He never beheld so fair a thing; trees along the river, beautiful and green and different from ours, with flowers and fruit after their own kind and little birds which sing very sweetly.

This was the big island—Cuba—where Columbus had hoped to find the Golden City. But if this were Marco Polo's island, Cipangu, what a liar Marco Polo was! Not a palace, no golden roofs, no golden streets—not even a decent house, was here. If Marco Polo had been truthful, then this wasn't Cipangu at all. Or perhaps the explorers must search another part of the island to find the wonders.

The voyage of discovery must have just begun.

CHAPTER EIGHT

Even though Columbus was deeply disappointed he appointed an embassy to pay a royal visit to the king. The Indians said in their often misunderstood sign language that the king was near.

When the emissaries returned they said they had seen only the same gentle, naked natives who were willing to give all they had, but there were no jewels or pearls or gold.

Columbus didn't stay depressed long. The men that were with him couldn't understand the faith that upheld him. He told them that there was another island, Babeque, where the natives gathered gold from the beaches by candlelight. He must set sail again.

"You are reckless. You are foolhardy," Martin Pinzón told him. Was that the way a captain should speak to his admiral? But Columbus knew what help this merchant mariner had been in gathering his crew at Palos and said as little as possible in anger.

November 19, Martin, in the fastest ship, the *Niña*, sailed off without permission. Would the *Pinta*, captained by Martin's brother, sail away, too, and leave the more awkward and slower *Santa María* to make it alone? No. The *Pinta* followed the *Santa María*.

Columbus thought, Martin wants to reach Babeque and fill his hold with treasure before we get there. And he wrote in his diary, "Many other things he has done and said to me."

On November 24 Columbus arrived at "Flat Island." The great trees made him dream of new world shipbuilding. At Baracoa Columbus dreamed of someday building a great city.

On December 5 he discovered Haiti. For the first time he was near the gold that would convince his sovereigns the whole expedition had not been a failure. He saw so much that reminded him of Spain that on December 12 he named the island Hispaniola.

Columbus loved beauty. In his journal he tried to paint in words the bold headlands, the deep forests, the singing of strange birds. He loved beauty wherever he saw it. He often saw it in the well-built bodies, the beautifully shaped heads, the great dark eyes of the young men he had seen since his first landing on San Salvadore. Now for the first time a young woman came aboard.

Columbus ordered his men to treat her with the greatest respect, and he gave her gifts from his trading materials. Of course an argument arose. Should they keep her on board or should they return her to the shore? By then the captive Indians were learning some Spanish. They were able to tell her that life on the boat was pleasant, and she told them that she wanted to stay. Columbus sent her ashore in the ship's boat.

Beautiful to all the men were the ornaments of gold that they saw the young natives wearing. Nearby there must be plenty of gold. Columbus thanked God for success.

Yet while he was writing about the gentleness and sweetness of the natives of Haiti, he was thinking that these kind, intelligent, willing people would make good slaves. Of course he knew that when the Bible spoke of "servants" it meant "slaves." He lived in a time when one man's ownership of another wasn't considered cruel. Yet how could Columbus, feeling himself a follower of Jesus, a servant of God, plan to enslave these friends?

On December 20 he landed at Santa Tomás. He saw so much beauty he ran out of words when he tried to describe it in his journal. Now he was certain that he was in Cathay.

Columbus seldom went on shore. He felt the place of an admiral was on the water. But he did land here and was surrounded by multitudes of men, women, and children. Though there were none of the silks and embroideries that Marco Polo had described, there were many more evidences of gold. On one of the banners he saw a symbol made of beaten gold. Here at last was something to take home to his sovereigns.

He thought he heard the natives say over and over again "Cibao." Surely this was their way of saying Cipangu, the island for which he had been searching. Never had he seen such friendly natives, and these were willing to trade gold for falcon's bells. For forty-eight hours every man on board the Spanish ships was busy doing business with the natives.

Finally, near midnight on Christmas Eve, Columbus spoke wearily to Juan de la Cosa and went to his cabin, prayed, and retired. Juan de la Cosa, too sleepy to stay awake, said a few words to the helmsman. The helmsman, finding his lids drooping and his mind wandering, turned the tiller over to the grummet. Columbus had absolutely forbidden this, but he was asleep and who would know?

The grummet heard the squeaking of the ship. He did not hear the sea pounding on a reef. The first thing he knew the *Santa María* was on a coral reef, sharper than knives, and the boy didn't know what else to do but shout.

Columbus came at once—the first one to the wheel. But it would take more than skill and prayer to free the *Santa María*. He ordered the cursing Juan de la Cosa to take to the ship's boat and help to free the ship from the reef. Juan de la Cosa took to the boat, all right. A group of Basque seamen went with him. They headed for the *Pinta* to save their own skins.

The captain of the *Pinta* wouldn't allow them to board. Instead he turned to help the *Santa María*. Finally Columbus and the others decided that the ship couldn't be saved. It must be unloaded and all cargo stored on land if possible.

Then the most dramatic event of the voyage occurred. Guacanagari, the native king, brought all of his canoes, and the men to operate them, to the side of the *Santa María*. Columbus's friend Las Casas said Guacanagari came not only to help but to "console the weeping admiral." He promised Columbus everything he owned to make up for the loss of the ship. The natives carried all the cargo safely to shore.

Once again Columbus's faith in the whole venture helped to overcome discouragement. He soon believed that the shipwreck had been predestined by God to give him a better chance to explore for the gold that would make more voyages of exploration possible. He wrote that such riches as he found here would certainly help the Christians to regain Jerusalem.

With the crews from both ships there were clearly too many men for the *Pinta*. Why not leave a garrison here until the next voyage? When Columbus spoke to the men about this idea everybody wanted to stay. Each man saw himself getting as much gold as possible while Columbus returned to Spain. It was the best of luck to be chosen to stay.

Material from the *Santa María* was used to build La Navidad. The makeshift fortress was stocked with supplies from the ship's hold. In charge was Diego de Haran, the cousin of Beatriz, mother of Columbus's son Ferdinand.

On January 4 Columbus, saying a good-bye to Guacanagari and the Spaniards who were staying on Hispaniola, started for Spain. Two days later a seaman, high on the rigging, sighted the *Niña*.

That evening the two ships anchored together, and Martin Alonzo came aboard the *Pinta*. He said that the parting was not his fault; that it was not planned. Columbus didn't believe a word of the explanation, but he was relieved to know that Martin Alonzo had been to Babeque and had not found gold. He had missed the gold that Columbus and his men had seen.

On January 16 the two ships, the *Pinta* and *Niña*, weighted anchor for the last time in the New World.

Columbus and Martin Alonzo didn't trust each other, didn't like each other, didn't even admire each other; but they were both glad that one ship would not have to face the wide Atlantic alone.

CHAPTER NINE

When the *Santa María*, the *Niña*, and the *Pinta* had been flying before the trade winds the crew had complained to Columbus, "How will we ever get back to Spain if the winds blow only one way?"

Columbus didn't know a great deal about winds, but he did know a lot about sailing. He chose a course that would put his two ships north of the trade winds. He had planned to stop at the Island of Women, home of the Amazons of ancient tales, but his men were anxious to get back to Spain so he set his course eastward without taking in the wood, water, and supplies he had hoped to pick up. "But the air [was] very soft and sweet as in Seville during April and May and the sea, many thanks to God, always very smooth."

By the evening of February 7 the smooth speed of the boats, pushed by the Westerlies, ended. But there were other winds and good weather: "May God be praised." On February 12 the weather changed, and the little armada moved right into a cyclone. "Now if the caravels hadn't been strong there would have been disaster...." Columbus was glad that the planks from the *Santa María* were in a fort in the New World instead of on the turbulent ocean. On February 14 *Pinta* was separated from *Niña* and, pushed by the fierce winds, disappeared.

"Stop steering a course," Columbus told his helmsman. "All we can hope to do is to stay afloat." Only God could save the ship.

The sailors, with their officers, now played a religious game. Lotteries were planned to select three men to go on pilgrimages if they came out of the storm alive. For each baptized Christian aboard a chick-pea was selected. In one was cut the symbol of the cross. Any man who drew out this special chick-pea would go on a pilgrimage to Santa María de Guadalupe in the mountains of Spain. Columbus put out his hand to select the first pea. The one he drew was the one with the symbol of the cross. "I am now a pilgrim and will fulfill my vows," he promised.

The peas were again shaken in the hat. This time Columbus didn't draw out the one with the cross. For the third time the peas were shaken. Again the admiral drew the special pea. He was now responsible to watch all night and to pay for a mass at the Church of Santa Clara de Maguar near Palos.

The waters were not stilled by these pilgrimage promises, so each Christian made a vow to "go in procession in their shirts" to the first shrine of the Virgin that they might reach. The men were sick with panic. No one expected to be alive to walk in this procession. The ship rocked and took on water as the planks groaned. Proud men vowed they were willing to put on the garment of the repentant sinner—do anything—if their lives could be saved.

When the storm was over Columbus was as penitent as anybody. Who had called him on this expedition? Who had brought him safely through every peril? Who intended that his discoveries would be a contribution to Christianity? God, of course. And yet in his weakness and anxiety his faith had faltered.

After their "day of the vows," the sea quieted somewhat and on February 15 the men sighted land. There were various guesses, but Columbus said "The Azores," and he was right.

Always more at home on the sea than land, Columbus now began to suffer with arthritis and was "much crippled in the legs." The plan had been to miss the Azores entirely, since they were owned by Portugal, but both ship and crew had taken such a beating in the storm that even Columbus was glad to cast anchor in the great bay.

After sunset three men appeared on a cliff overlooking the bay. Columbus sent out the ship's boat, and the men came aboard bringing fresh bread and chickens. Never were guests better received. The visitors said that there was a shrine to the Virgin Mary near the sea. Columbus remembered the vow all the men had made to wear only their shirts in penance and walk to the shrine.

Of course all the men couldn't go at once. Columbus sent half the crew, waiting himself to go with the second group. The men took off their shoes, their hose, their pants, and wearing only their shirts marched to the shrine. What an opportunity for the men of the little town! They seized the Spaniards while they were praying and threw them into prison.

The real captain of the little island was away and in his place was a young man who must have dreamed great dreams. This young fellow said he was following the orders of King John of Portugal who had been annoyed by Castilians on the coast of Guinea where they didn't belong.

Columbus couldn't see the town from where the ship was anchored so he lifted anchor and sailed the *Niña* to a better vantage point. He saw many men gathered on horseback. He saw that the men were armed and that they intended to come by boat to the ship.

It didn't take a mind reader to know that the men had been instructed to capture Columbus. Columbus intended to counter by getting the young official on board and holding him as hostage. Columbus wouldn't land, and the official wouldn't come aboard. Columbus showed his passport and ship's papers, but the young official wouldn't come close enough to read them. Finally Columbus, generally very gentle of speech, lost his patience. "I am Admiral of the Ocean Sea and Viceroy to the Indies. I am sailing back to Castile though I have only half a crew, and I'll see that you are properly punished."

"This is Portugal. Where is Castile?"

"I swear by San Fernando I'm not leaving this place until I have a hundred Portuguese to carry home as slaves." Columbus sailed back to his first anchorage.

February 22 Columbus returned to the little village and his shirt-tailed crew was returned to him by boat. But it was February 24 before the winds let him sail toward home.

Viceroy—a ruler exercising athority in a colony on behalf of a sovereign.

No sooner were Columbus and his crew free of the island than another storm overtook them, and they were fortunate to make the mouth of the Taugus River. The storms they had encountered on the Atlantic were not as fierce and dangerous as those they battled between the Azores and Portugal.

Columbus hadn't wanted to enter Portugal at all. Now he gratefully crossed the bar into the Taugus River because he "could do nothing else."

The first fisherman who saw the *Niña* made prayers for her all morning. Many ships had been lost in the wild weather.

Columbus had not the slightest desire to see King John, who had twice rejected him and his plans. But if he were Admiral of the Ocean Sea and Viceroy of the Indies, he must act the part. He wrote a note to King John, asking permission to sail up the Taugus River to safety.

Moored next to the little *Niña* was a man-of-war. The master of this great ship was Bartholomew Dias who had discovered the Cape of Good Hope. In a fully armed boat he sailed to the *Niña*, boarded, and demanded that Columbus give an account of himself.

"I am Admiral of the Ocean Sea and Viceroy of India. If I leave this ship it will be because I have been removed by force of arms." Bartholomew, defeated by Columbus's dignity and courage, returned to his ship. When he reported to the captain of the ship what had happened, the captain paid a visit of state to the Admiral of the Ocean Sea with an escort of pipers and drummers.

In Portugal everyone was eager to see Columbus and

the natives who had returned with him. People on the streets thanked God "for the great and good increase of Christianity."

King John sent a message inviting Columbus to court. It was unthinkable to say no, yet certainly there was danger in saying yes. Columbus selected some gold ear plugs to show that there was wealth in the newly discovered land and the healthiest Indians to prove that he had been to an undiscovered land and not to the coast of Africa. Columbus and his party left by mule for the monastery in which King John was staying to escape the plague that was ravaging the cities.

Lisbon had been home to Columbus. Here he had met and married Dona Felipe; here Diego had been born; and here Dona was buried, but Columbus didn't comment on his feelings on being in Lisbon in his journal.

And so King John and Columbus met again. Columbus was forty-two; the king, thirty-eight. John received him graciously but must have regretted that Columbus had not sailed for Portugal and taken all these new lands in the name of his crown.

Columbus didn't feel comfortable even when King John "spoke fair." Perhaps, he thought, John was insincere and only waited for a better time to do him harm. And now that he was spending so much time in Portugal the *Pinta* would probably reach Spain first and Martin Alonzo Pinzón would take credit for all of the discoveries. At last Columbus convinced King John that he had not gone to any part of Guinea.

Columbus boasted that the Indians were highly intelligent. King John arranged a sort of intelligence test. He had a bag of beans put on the table. He scattered the beans and asked the Indians to make a map of the lands that Columbus had discovered. The dark hands moved quickly. There was Hispaniola, there, Cuba. The single bean was the Bahamas and another bean stood for the Lesser Antilles.

The king mixed the beans up and commanded another Indian to reassemble them. This time the map was in greater detail. Now King John knew how much land Columbus had taken in the name of the Royal Sovereigns of Spain—land that might have been his if he had listened to Columbus. Although the king's advisers urged him to have Columbus assassinated he didn't take their advice. He allowed Columbus to return to the *Niña*. When the *Niña* was ready to sail he sent a royal messenger to suggest that Columbus go by land accompanied by the royal messenger who would take care of all arrangements.

Was King John offering a courtesy or hoping to lure Columbus to a mountainous country where he could be assassinated? Columbus didn't know the answer to this question, but he quickly said, "An admiral's place is on the water!"

On March 13 the *Niña* crew weighed anchor and were off for Palos.

CHAPTER TEN

Just thirty-two weeks from the day that Columbus's little armada had left Palos, the *Niña* slipped into harbor. What rejoicing!

Columbus wrote: "Of this voyage I observe that it . . . will be to the greater glory of Christianity, which to some slight extent has already occurred." Columbus finished with these words his remarkable day-to-day journal of the first voyage. But he wasn't finished with writing. He must send a message to the royal highnesses at once or Martin Alonzo Pinzón would make the first report of the remarkable discovery. Columbus had already sent a letter from Lisbon but it might have been lost, so he sent another letter by way of Seville to Barcelona where the court was staying.

Indeed Martin Alonzo Pinzón had sent the first letter to the royal sovereigns since he had arrived in Portugal before Columbus in the fast caravel, the *Pinta*. The sovereigns had answered that they preferred to get the report from the admiral.

The day that Columbus reached Palos the same tide

brought in the *Pinta*. Through a miscalculation she had first reached land four hundred and fifty miles from Palos. Martin Alonzo, who had probably been the first to see the mainland of America, surely the first to sight Haiti, was so ill he didn't stop to make sure his sails were furled or to report to the flagship. He went to his home in Palos and died.

Now everywhere there was celebration. Each member of the crew of the *Niña* and *Pinta* was a hero. There were banquets and festivals, not only in Palos but in the towns up and down the coast that could claim fame because of an exploring son.

But Columbus was restless in the celebration. He had written the royal sovereigns that he would expect a reply to his letter when he reached Seville. Since he had selected the chick-pea with the cross on it, before he left for Seville he performed his vows at Santa Clara de Moguer and Santa Maria de la Cinta, and spent two weeks with Fray Juan Pérez at La Rábida.

Then, taking ten Indians with him, he traveled to Seville, arriving during Holy Week. In Seville there were daily processions of monks carrying statues of the saints through the streets and ceremonies in the Cathedral. Finally there was Easter morning. Columbus felt that his exploration, done in the sight of God and with His help, had been a religious experience.

The next day he received the royal sovereigns' letter:

We have seen your letters and we have taken much pleasure in learning whereof you write, and that God gave so good a result to your labors, and well guided you in what you commenced, whereof He will be served and we also, and our realms receive so much advantage. . . . It will please God that, beyond that wherein you serve Him, you should receive from us many favors. . . . Inasmuch as we will that that which you have commenced with the aid of God be continued and furthered, and we desire that you 'come here forthwith, therefore for our service make the best haste you can in your coming, so that you may be timely provided with everything you need; and because as you see the summer has begun, and you must not delay in going back there, see if something can be prepared in Seville or in other districts for your returning to the land which you have discovered. And write us at once in this mail which departs presently, so that things may be provided as well as may be, while you are coming and returning, in such manner that when you return hence, all will be ready. From Barcelona on the 30th day of March 1493. I the King   I the Queen

Columbus couldn't have been happier. He wasn't going to be required to present proof of anything. And already the royal sovereigns were planning on a second voyage. At once Columbus wrote his idea of how colonization of the new lands should be carried out. Perhaps he had been planning this memorial for a long time. Most of it was wise.

He didn't want to start with too many men. Two thousand would be enough. The two thousand volunteers should be settled in three or four towns and each town should have civic officers, a church, and a priest. The priest was to say mass, conduct services, and convert the Indians. Columbus wasn't forgetting the first purpose of his exploration, to preach Christ to "every kindred, tongue, and people."

But while he was thinking of the conversion of the Indians he knew that volunteers for the expedition would be thinking of gold. He limited the men who could seek gold to those who had built houses in planned towns. Everyone who found gold must hand it over to the town clerk who would weigh it and make it into bars, specially stamped. Half of all gold found must go to the crown, 1 percent to the church.

There was one serious weakness in Columbus's plan. Anyone who wished to make further discoveries could do so. He didn't dream, then, of the terrible trouble this would cause. The rule seemed fair enough.

Columbus sent the letter by fast messenger, then he followed with six Indians, a few servants, and an officer from the first journey.

The people came out to see Columbus with his group of strange Indians as he passed through the blossoming fields and orchards bound for Barcelona.

Columbus loved Cordova and felt it was his home. His sons, Diego and Ferdinand, were there. Beatriz, the mother of Ferdinand, was there. But more important, the royal sovereigns were waiting to greet him in Barcelona. He must hurry on.

The king and queen received him in the great alcazar. When he approached they stood up to greet him. When he knelt in the usual manner they invited him to rise and sit beside them. They talked for an hour about his discoveries and then all went to the royal chapel. When the *Te Deum* was chanted Columbus felt tears running down his cheeks. He stole a look at the royal sovereigns. They were weeping, too. Never had Columbus felt God's Spirit more strongly.

For five or six weeks Columbus stayed in Barcelona.

The big event to him was the baptizing of the Indians. He not only attended religious ceremonies but went to banquet after banquet. The royal sovereigns gave him the right to use the gold castle of Castile and the purple lily of León on his coat of arms. They promised that his son, Diego, and Diego's descendants would inherit the title of Admiral of the Ocean Sea and Viceroy of all the lands Columbus should discover.

Columbus had achieved fame, but he was aching to get on with another voyage. He was sure that he had just begun the work God wanted him to do.

CHAPTER ELEVEN

How difficult it had been to prepare the *Santa María*, the *Niña*, and the *Pinta* for the first voyage into the unknown! In March of 1493 how easy it was to start preparations for a much greater armada for the second venture.

Columbus was made Captain General of the Fleet, and Don Juan de Fonseca was made jointly responsible for preparations. Fonseca was a good businessman and organizer. Columbus could leave most of the work to him. There were to be seventeen vessels ranging in size from the flagship to vessels not much bigger than launches which would be suitable for river and bay exploration. Each vessel had to be equipped with food and arms and other supplies. Columbus had been on two trips to the Portuguese mines in Africa, and he knew that Europeans couldn't live on the food to be found in newly discovered lands. He had enjoyed the sweet potatoes on his first voyage, but twelve or fifteen hundred men would need more than sweet potatoes.

Besides these supplies Columbus wanted seeds, plants,

tools, and animals to start farming communities.

In May 1493 the royal sovereigns issued instructions to Columbus. The prime purpose of the voyage was to bring Christ to the Indians; the second purpose was to establish trading colonies. For the Christianizing of the natives Fray Buel and other religious men would go with the fleet. Columbus must see that the Indians were "treated very well and lovingly." Any Europeans who injured the Indians should be punished.

It wasn't until June 1493 that Columbus was allowed to leave Barcelona. Fonseca was in Seville working on the preparation of the fleet, but Columbus didn't go directly to Seville.

When he had drawn the special chick-pea the night of the great hurricane he had vowed to go to the Monastery of Guadalupe and worship at the shrine of the Virgin there. The image of the Virgin of Guadalupe was said to have been carved by St. Luke himself. The pilgrimage took Columbus more than one hundred and thirty extra miles—a long way to travel on the back of a mule.

At Cordova he said good-bye to Beatriz and, taking his two young sons with him, pushed on to Seville. There he found fault with everything Fonseca had done. At Cadiz he was especially disappointed that his armada wouldn't be ready to sail by mid-August.

The flagship, like the one of the first voyage, was named *Santa María*, then nicknamed *Mariagalante*. The *Niña* which had done so well on the first voyage was in the new armada.

While it had been almost impossible to get men for the first voyage, now everyone wanted to go. The shipmates of the original trip were given first chance. There were over twelve hundred men, but not one woman. Of all the men on board, the one Columbus trusted most was his younger brother, Diego. His two sons didn't go with him, but they waved from the shore when the cannon roared and the bands played and the fleet "so handsome and united" sailed for the Canaries.

Fresh supplies were taken on at Gomera where Columbus had stopped on his first voyage and about October 13 the fleet weighed anchor and was off for the Indies.

Columbus didn't sail directly to Hispaniola but planned to take a look at the islands to the southeast. He charted his course well and cut a week of sailing time from the Canaries to landfall.

The trip was uneventful. The islands to which Columbus directed the fleet were beautiful. The only unfortunate thing about them was that they were peopled not by the gentle Arawak Indians he had traded with before but by the Caribs (Carib is the root of cannibal). On one island the Caribs fled when a party of Spaniards came to the shore in the ship's boat. What the men were planning to do on the island isn't known; whatever it was, they didn't do it. Instead they became hopelessly lost.

When they didn't return to the ship Columbus sent out four searching parties of fifty men each. Even two hundred men couldn't find the lost party, but they did find something that made them sick. In the empty huts from which the Caribs had fled they found large cuts of human flesh, boys who were being fattened for food, and girls who were kept to produce babies—a food the Caribs particularly enjoyed.

The men freed the Arawak captives and took them back to ship. They even captured some Caribs.

"We'll leave tomorrow whether we find our lost comrades or not," Columbus decided. But that evening the lost party started a fire on a mountain peak. The fire was seen from the shore, and the lost men were rescued.

Columbus was so sickened by the diet of the Caribs that he ordered every one of their canoes to be destroyed. The Caribs couldn't raid the Arawaks without boats.

The men brought on board twelve "very beautiful and plump" girls fifteen or sixteen years old.

* * *

Columbus gave a name to each island he discovered, but he didn't plan to colonize any of them though they were beautiful beyond description. He didn't allow anyone ashore since he didn't want to spend days searching for another lost party.

At one island he called Santa Cruz the Europeans had their first fight with the natives—a fight that could have been easily avoided.

It was about noon when a party of the armada entered a small estuary on Santa Cruz. Columbus needed water, so he sent a group of men and empty water barrels to the shore on the ship's boat. The boat was armed because the Caribs were dangerous. When the men landed the Caribs disappeared into the forest, leaving some Arawak girls and boys behind. Columbus's men freed the Arawaks who were probably being fattened for eating and decided to take them back to the ship.

Down the west coast came a boat carrying four men, two women, and a boy. Instead of going on to the ship and minding their own business, the Spaniards moved their boat so as to cut off the Caribs' escape. Although there were twenty-five men on the ship's boat and only seven in the canoe the Caribs decided to fight. Two Spaniards were killed, the Caribs were killed or captured, and the Arawak prisoners swam out to the Spanish ships begging to be taken aboard. Anything was better than being prisoners of the Caribs.

From this Bay of Arrows the armada went north to the Virgin Islands. The small vessels explored the coast while the larger ones kept to the outer waterway. Columbus thought the island of Puerto Rico to be as large as Sicily, but he made no effort to explore it; he was too eager to reach Navidad. How had the small colony of men made out since he had left them on the first voyage? When they reached Hispaniola a party went ashore at Monte Cristo to look for a possible place for a town. Here they found two decaying bodies tied with ropes. One of the bodies had a heavy beard. Since Indians didn't have beards, this had to be a Spaniard!

Columbus was all the more eager to get to Cape Hatien and Navidad. The ships reached there that night. Remembering what had happened to the *Santa María*, he anchored outside the reef. He ordered the guns to be fired. No answering fire came. He ordered flares to be lighted. No answering flares were sent up.

Early in the morning an Indian came out but refused to board ship until he recognized Columbus. The Indian was a cousin of Guacanagari, Columbus's friend. He brought two golden masks—one for Columbus and one for Martin Alonzo Pinzón (who had died soon after his return to Palos).

"The Christians are well," he said through Diego Colon, the interpreter. "Some died of illness. Some killed each other in a quarrel."

"And where is Guacanagari?"

"Wounded in a fight with another cacique—a fight to defend your men."

When the conversation with Columbus was over the Indian continued to talk with Diego Colon. Not a Christian was left alive, he said. When the Indians had left in their canoe Diego told Columbus this news. The admiral could not believe it. These were such kind Indians—so meek, so timid; and the forty Spaniards were armed, aggressive, and strong.

The crew watched through the night. The first light of dawn showed nothing left of the fortress that had been built at Navidad. When Guacanagari's cousin came aboard the next day he admitted that not one Christian still lived.

"Where is Guacanagari? He must come to me and explain this tragedy," Columbus said.

But when Guacanagari did not come the next day Columbus and his physician, Dr. Chanca, found in the huts on the shore many articles that had belonged to the forty dead Spaniards. And these were huts belonging to the Arawaks, not to some Carib tribe.

Near where the first bodies had been seen the Indians showed them eleven more bodies, lying where they had fallen. Caonabo, another cacique, had killed them, they insisted. It was Caonabo who had wounded Guacanagari.

Diego Colon, listening to the Indians talking with each other, heard far more than he was expected to interpret. The Christians, they said, had done them all manner of harm.

In spite of the sorrow and disappointment, Columbus was determined to establish four new colonies. He sent out men to find suitable sites. Maldonado visited Guacanagari and found him stretched on a hammock. His thigh, he said, was wounded by Caonabo, who had killed all the Christians.

When Columbus heard this report he organized a procession of a hundred. Dressed in their brightest clothing and with banners flying they marched to the music of fife and drum to the hut of Cacique Guacanagari. Dr. Chanca said he had come to dress the wound. When he unrolled the bandages he found no wound.

When Columbus and his men held a council Fray Buel, who had been named to convert the Indians, said, "We must kill this deceitful cacique. His death would be an example to the others."

Columbus knew men as Fray Buel knew Latin masses. "Guacanagari isn't guilty. How can you judge him without hearing his story?"

They decided to do nothing while they were still crazed with anger and shock.

It did not take long to find out the truth. The

Spaniards had disobeyed Columbus's orders about treatment of the Indians. They had decided to form groups to search for gold. One group got into the territory of Caonabo who was a Carib by birth. In revenge, Caonabo organized a group to assault the fort. There were only ten men under the direction of Diego de Harana in the fort, and they were easily defeated. It was true that Guacanagari had tried to help Diego de Harana. Several of his men had been wounded by the fish-bone spear heads of Caonabo.

Why hadn't the Spaniards behaved themselves? Why had they stolen from the Indians? Why had they raped the Indian women? Was this any way to Christianize the natives of a new land?

On the second voyage Columbus had already discovered twenty large islands and even more small ones. But he had also discovered that men, freed from the eye of authority and hungry for gold, were not good emissaries for Christ.

CHAPTER TWELVE

The tragedy at Navidad upset all Columbus's plans. Navidad was supposed to have been the center for Spanish colonization. The settlers there were supposed to have found the source of gold and have barrels of it ready for export to Spain.

Now there was nothing.

Temporarily, at least, Columbus had to forget Christianizing the natives who had seen all too clearly what sort of men Christians could be. He had two big tasks to perform: to start colonization and—if he was to continue his explorations—to find gold.

On January 2, 1494, he anchored his fleet near a wooded plain. Here he founded Isabela. He had chosen a poor site. There was no harbor, no drinking water within a mile, and no gold, though the natives said gold was near. But his livestock were dying, half his men were sick, and the weather was terrible.

To find gold Columbus organized an expedition under the leadership of Alonzo de Hojeda. Columbus might have known this firebrand well when he spent time with the Duke of Medina Celi, since the Duke was also the patron of Hojeda. The party was gone from Isabela just two weeks and returned with gold nuggets, some large, some small, and with gold hammered into sheets.

At first Columbus thought he should keep the seventeen ships with him until he could send them back to Spain loaded with gold. But the men were sick, restless, and hungry. Columbus guessed that the problem was lack of familiar food, and Dr. Chanca needed more medicine. He wrote: "Under God the preservation of their health depends upon these people being provided with the provisions they are used to in Spain."

He kept five vessels with him and sent twelve back to Spain. In the vessels he sent the gold that was available, spices, parrots, and twenty-six Indians. The Indians, though unwilling, were to learn Spanish and become Christians. Most important was a letter asking for supplies as soon as possible. The returning fleet made the trip in twenty-five days, and the royal sovereigns were pleased with the report Columbus had sent.

Columbus left Isabela for a land expedition March 12, 1494. Flags were flying, fifes blaring, drums beating. With his entourage he passed through the mountains and into a great valley that looked like a garden. In the black moist soil of the valley grass and flowers grew in profusion. The natives came from their huts bringing gifts of food and gold dust. These gentle people gave all they had and couldn't understand when the Spaniards didn't return their kindness.

Sunday, March 15, the expedition crossed the valley, and Columbus selected a site for a fort. Santo Tomás was built to house and protect the fifty men Columbus would leave there. He planned to make this the center of his mining operations. There hadn't been any gold in the valley, but there was plenty in the mountains. He put Mosen Pedro Margarit in charge of a company of prospectors with instructions to live off the land. Hojeda was to be in charge of the whole operation.

After an exploring trip of nearly a month Columbus and most of the men returned to Isabela. The crops had done well—very well—but the men were near mutiny. Columbus selected four hundred men, including the troublemakers, and sent them out to Hojeda to explore for gold. Hojeda didn't have the personality or character to lead a peaceful expedition. He heard the Indians had stopped three Spaniards who were traveling from Santo Tomás to Isabela and had stolen some bright clothing to give to their cacique. These were the Indians who had given all they possessed to the Spaniards when they greeted them. But now Hojeda cut off the ears of one of the Indians and sent the cacique with his brother and nephew to Isabela. Another cacique who had helped Columbus went with them. When he begged for the lives of the three Indians, Columbus freed them—but the harm already had been done.

The garrison at Navidad had been wiped out because of the wrongdoing of the Spaniards and now the dignity, if not the lives, of these natives had been destroyed because of a few old clothes.

Columbus was never happy or effective on land. Ciboa was not Cipangu (Japan). Perhaps it was Sheba. Anyway it was an island, not mainland Asia, and he must get on with his search.

He left April 24 with three ships, the *Niña*, *San Juan*, and *Cardera*, to find something good to report when the supply ships returned from Spain. Isabela he left in charge of a council which included Fray Buel and his brother, Diego. After a long, slow voyage he reached Cuba, which he called Juana. He set up a column topped with a cross and took the land in the name of Spain. This he had already done on the first voyage.

Columbus was sure that Cuba was a peninsula of Asia. With his three ships he explored the south coast. The ships put in at Guantanamo Bay. Columbus called it Puerto Grande. As he sailed westward from Guantanamo the natives swam out with gifts. Diego Colon interpreted their cries: "Eat and drink, men from heaven."

The natives had described a land of gold called Jameque. Columbus thought they meant Babeque of which he had heard so often on his first voyage. He deserted his exploration of the coast of Cuba for Jamaica.

As usual Columbus was entranced with beauty. Jamaica was beautiful. The men were more interested in the enormous canoes they saw being used. The natives on the north coast of Jamaica were unfriendly and Columbus turned back toward Cuba. For a time the voyage was pleasant; then came problems. The ships threaded their way between islands, sometimes with their bottoms dragging in soft sand. Columbus was so sure that he was skirting the coast of Asia that he even made plans for going back to Spain by way of the Cape of Good Hope. He thought he might even stop at the Red Sea and go on a pilgrimage to Jerusalem and Rome!

On May 28 he anchored off a very large grove where there was plenty of fresh water. Here a very strange thing took place. One of the crossbowmen who went hunting for food in the woods came upon a band of about thirty Indians. With them was a white man dressed in a long white robe. The crossbowman thought for a minute that this was the friar from one of the Spanish ships. Then there appeared with him two other white men in short tunics that ended at the knees. The bowman was so frightened that he ran for the beach, not waiting to hear what the men had to say. When he looked around from a safe point the three had disappeared.

Columbus listened to the story. Perhaps the man in the white robe was Prester John who, according to legend, lived in Ethiopia or India. He now was certain that the islands he was passing through were part of the Malay Archipelago. Cuba must be the Chinese province of Mangi and the shore southward was the beginning of the Malay Peninsula. But it was time to go back to Isabela. Had he gone fifty miles up the coast of Cuba he would have known it to be an island.

The weather as he turned back toward Isabela was so bad, the winds so adverse, he just couldn't travel. Why not go on with the exploration of Jamaica?

This time he would look at the south coast. He found the natives there friendly, completely unlike those on the north coast.

He made plans, after circumnavigating Jamaica, to explore the south coast of Hispaniola. But every day he grew more weary. The diet was poor, and there had been so many navigational problems that he had often gone as long as eight days with less than three hours sleep. One day he was too ill to take command. His fever was high, and he couldn't see. Perhaps if he stayed in his cabin he would be better. He didn't regain his sight; instead he lost his other senses one by one. Eventually he couldn't remember where he was or what he was doing; then he could no longer speak.

His crew was terrified. Instead of going on with the exploration they turned toward Isabela. It was September 29 when they anchored near Isabela and carried Columbus ashore.

He had not found gold or pearls or the cities of the Orient. He had circumnavigated Jamaica, explored the south coast of Cuba, and seen more of the south coast of Hispaniola. What did all that matter if he were dying?

But at Isabela he could rest. And rest he did—for five months.

CHAPTER THIRTEEN

When Columbus was carried from the ship by
frightened seamen his brother Bartholomew was there
to greet him. Diego hadn't been a successful adminis-
trator. He lacked the qualities of leadership and drive
which Columbus exhibited—at least on the sea—but
Bartholomew had all the qualities that his younger
brother lacked. He had been in England and France
when Columbus had left on his first voyage. He had
hurried to Spain to make the second voyage but he
had arrived too late. When Columbus sent twelve ships
home for supplies Bartholomew had sailed in charge of
the returning armada.

As soon as Columbus was well enough to speak he
made Bartholomew the chief officer. The office needed
a loyal man of action like Bartholomew, not a priestly
type like Diego.

Before Columbus had left on his exploring expedition
he had given Hojeda and Mosen Pedro Margarit too
much power and too much freedom. Columbus himself
had been consistently kind to the Indians. He was by
nature a gentle person, and he had instructed the other

Christians to act in the same way. They hadn't, of course. He had told them, "Their highnesses desire more the salvation of these people by making them Christians than all the riches that can be obtained from them." But the adventurers left in charge did not share this desire.

Hojeda commanded the fort of Santa Tomás. Margarit and his hidalgos, crossbowmen, musketeers, and troopers ranged the countryside. They demanded food and gold. The Indians gave all they had, but when there was no more to give the Spanish whipped them, stole their wives and daughters, and made slaves of their sons.

The caciques—all but Guacanagari—and their subjects grew enraged and went to Diego with their grievances. Diego wrote to Margarit and told him to change his ways. The letter made Margarit so angry that he took the three ships Bartholomew had just brought from Spain and sailed back to Spain to complain. With him went Fray Buel and most of the priests who were supposed to have begun the Christianizing of the Indians. One who stayed was Fray Ramón Pane who baptized the first Indian in the New World in 1496.

When Columbus came back to Isabela the three ships had already sailed and everything was in chaos. The men whom Margarit had deserted were without supplies or discipline. They roamed the island, killing and stealing. The Indians, once so friendly, killed in return.

Columbus had a serious problem. Queen Isabella had told him to see that the Indians were "treated well and lovingly." This he had always tried to do, even insisting that Indians who had given his men gifts should receive trading truck in return. But what should he do now? He asked himself "Which are better? Christians or pagans?" The answer was "Christians, of course." Therefore Indians shouldn't defend themselves against the Spaniards. Therefore he allowed horses and hounds to round up fifteen hundred natives to be punished instead of punishing Margarit's outlaws.

One day in September Antonio de Torres arrived at Isabela with four caravels of provisions. He also brought a letter from the royal sovereigns asking Columbus to return to Spain for a conference with them. If that would be too difficult he should send his brother or some other person who knew about the new islands to help them to come to an agreement with Portugal on the ownership of the new lands.

Columbus knew that Margarit and Fray Buel would soon be at the court and it might be well for him to be there to present his side of the story, but he felt that staying in Hispaniola was more important than drawing a line of demarcation between Spanish and Portuguese possessions or of defending himself against the slander of malcontents.

The caravels must go back, of course. There was little gold to send. No one had discovered any gold mines. There was little fine cotton cloth. What else was there of value? The Spaniards didn't like the wood or the spices. Slaves! Columbus could send Indians into slavery. He could capture the Caribs who were the enemies of the gentle Arawaks. That would really be doing a fine thing for the Caribs. Wouldn't they learn the Spanish language, become Christians, and give up their habit of eating human flesh?

But the Arawaks were easier to capture, and it was these formerly friendly people who were packed into the ships to be sold into slavery.

With the caravels sailed Diego who would represent his brother against the lies and slanders of Fray Buel and Margarit. The poor Indians suffered immeasurably. More than two hundred died during the voyage and were thrown into the sea. The others, offered for sale by Fonseca, were naked in the colder air of Spain and died quickly.

The caciques in Hispaniola were desperate. They tried to unite against the Spaniards of Isabela and push them into the sea, but two hundred Spaniards with horses and hounds made the Indians panic.

Still Caonabo, who had destroyed Navidad, was free. Hojeda took just two men to visit Caonabo. He showed the cacique a pair of handcuffs and foot fetters. They were new and of burnished copper. "These are such as Spanish kings wear at festivals," Hojeda told the cacique. "Since you are ruler of your people you should try them on. Would you like to?"

Caonabo said that he would. Riding behind Hojeda, his body bound to the Spaniard's, Caonabo was taken to Isabela. Hojeda was then sent to capture Caonabo's brother. This was more difficult. The Spaniards now subdued the entire island. Gone was the golden age that Columbus had interrupted with his first voyage. Now a Spaniard could go anywhere in safety. Subduing the island had taken from May 1495 to March 1496.

In October 1495 before the island had been completely subjugated, four caravels came from Spain under the command of Juan Aguado. He had been in Hispaniola with Columbus but had gone back to Spain with Torres. Now he was charged by the royal sovereigns with investigating Columbus's successes and failures as a governor.

It really was time for Columbus to go back to Spain and speak for himself. Before he left he gave his brother, Bartholomew, instructions to abandon Isabela and build a new city at a better site. The new city was to be Santa Domingo.

CHAPTER FOURTEEN

The trip back to Spain was long and hazardous. The *Niña* and the *India*, built to accommodate twenty-five to thirty each, now carried two hundred and fifty Christians and thirty Indians. The Spaniards had learned from the natives how to make cassava bread, but on the long voyage even that ran so low that each man had one piece with a single cup of water each day. Some suggested that it would save food to throw the Indians overboard. Others even suggested that the Indians should be eaten. But Columbus, always a better commander on water than on land, declared that the Caribs were human beings and should be treated as such.

Finally they reached Portugal, and eventually the pathetic armada, with flags flying, eased into the Bay of Cadiz.

When Columbus arrived at Cadiz he put on the coarse brown habit of a Franciscan friar—proof that he repented of his weaknesses and was humble, not proud as he had been between his first and second voyages. His closest friends were now monks and friars.

He lived at the home of a curate until he received an invitation from the royal sovereigns to come to court.

Court was now a hundred miles north of Madrid but Columbus, fed and rested, started bravely with a small cavalcade. With him were the brother and nephew of Caonabo. (Caonabo had died at sea.) He also had the rest of the Indians who, he thought, could learn Spanish, then Christianity, and become missionaries to the Indians. There were also bright-colored parrots in cages. When the cavalcade moved through a town the Indians were decked in jewelry that showed the townspeople that Columbus had discovered gold, not just an alloy as his enemies had said.

At Guadalupe some of the Indians were baptized, then Columbus hurried on. He wanted to see the royal sovereigns, of course, but he was even more anxious to see his sons, Diego and Ferdinand, who were now pages to Crown Prince Don Juan.

The royal sovereigns greeted him graciously. He gave them the Indians, the parrots, the gold jewelry, nuggets, and dust. Ferdinand and Isabella listened to his report. They seemed to have paid little attention to the lies his enemies had told about him.

Columbus asked for eight ships for a third voyage, and the royal sovereigns agreed. Two would go immediately to Hispaniola with supplies; six would go with him to discover the mainland that Columbus was still sure was Cathay. But Ferdinand and Isabella were busy arranging royal marriages. Don Juan was to marry the Archduchess Margarita of Austria; Dona Juana, Archduke Philip of Hapsburg; and Dona

Isabella, Manual, King of Portugal. These weddings took time, money, and ships for royal escort.

April 3, 1497, the royal sovereigns finally got around to issuing orders for the third voyage. Only three hundred and fifty men and boys were to go, in contrast to the fifteen hundred on the second voyage. Thirty women were to go without pay. They were expected to earn their own way. In an order issued June 5, 1497, Columbus was told to engage priests to administer the holy sacraments and "convert the Indians. . . to our Holy Catholic Faith."

Because people were no longer anxious to go on these adventures, prisoners who had not committed grave crimes were permitted to go if they wished, thus winning pardons.

Columbus had all the official sanction he needed, but what he really needed was the cooperation of Don Juan de Fonseca who had charge of getting the ships and men ready. This he didn't have. Fonseca said he needed money, and this the royal sovereigns didn't have, what with the expense of wars, marriages, and negotiations.

First *Niña* and *India* sailed for Hispaniola with provisions for the settlement. Columbus sent a letter to his brother saying that he had "never experienced such anxieties and obstacles." But at last in May 1498 Columbus sailed with six ships. He knew exactly where he was going. He expected to find a continent on the equator, or at least south of the Antilles. Aristotle had said that "gold and things of value" were to be found where the people were black or tan and the temperature was very hot. Columbus knew that if he

87

didn't find gold and jewels this time the royal sovereigns' interest in his discoveries would run out, the colonists at Hispaniola would be forgotten, and the natives would remain unchristianized.

On July 4, 1498, the rest of the fleet took off from the Canaries. But Columbus didn't plan to follow the *Niña* and *India*. To find the expected continent near the equator he would have to go much farther south. He thought of Guinea on the west coast of Africa. How rich the Portuguese had found it! He would go south as far as Guinea—to about the tenth parallel— then change his course to straight west. He could not follow the African coast to Guinea, of course. That would cause him to lose time, and the Portuguese would be most unfriendly.

He did not know what he would find, but he hoped for riches. If he didn't strike this dreamed-of land before he reached a point south of Hispaniola he could then sail directly north to familiar territory.

The plan was good and the rich land he envisioned was really there, but Columbus didn't know about winds and ocean currents. This course led him directly into a calm where the fleet spent eight days in insufferable heat. It was fortunate that only one day was sunny. The overcast skies and frequent showers saved the lives of his men.

On July 22 a sudden wind arose and filled the sails. At noon on July 31 a seaman climbed to the crow's nest and saw the three hills which Columbus immediately named Trinidad (for the Holy Trinity).

Only one barrel of water was left so he looked for a place where a river emptied into the ocean. He found just such a spot; the men filled their casks and drank, then stripped and swam in the cool water. They saw no people but their spirits were raised.

August 1, 1498, a highlight of the trip occurred but neither Columbus nor his men knew it. They sighted the mainland of America (Venezuela). Columbus who had thought Cuba to be a continent now thought the mainland was an island. It seemed too far away to investigate immediately so the fleet anchored at Trinidad.

On August 5 the fleet anchored and the boats went ashore on the mainland of America. This was a memorable occasion—the first landing of Europeans on the American continent! Here there were fish, fruit, fire, people, a "great house," and monkeys. They were on the Paria Peninsula. However, since the wind was good they soon left and sailed up the coast to take possession of the land. Columbus's eyes were so inflamed and sore that he sent Captain Pedro de Terreros "with a sword in one hand and a banner in the other" to take the land in the name of the royal sovereigns and to raise a great cross.

Here Columbus discovered a new culture. The Indians worked gold with copper and silver to make an alloy usable with less heat in smelting. There were great freighting canoes with cabins amidship. There were large houses with seats for many guests. And best of all there were pearls. The natives wore necklaces of pearls and seeds.

Yet Columbus didn't stay on Paria, thinking he could come back to the pearl coast later. He left to return to Hispaniola. From this time on he was more blamed for what he didn't see than praised for what he saw.

He wrote:

> And your highnesses will win these lands which are another world, and where Christianity will have so much enjoyment, and our faith, in time so great an increase. All this I say with very honest intent and because I desire your Highnesses may be the greatest lords in the world, lords of it all, I say; and that all be with much service to and satisfaction of the Holy Trinity.

But who in Spain would believe this prophecy?

CHAPTER FIFTEEN

Leaving behind him the continent which he had been so eager to discover, Columbus followed a course westward along the Paria Peninsula. He began to wonder if this weren't indeed part of a continent. Where was all the fresh water coming from if this were an island? Never in his experience had he seen so much fresh water pouring into the sea. But never in his experience had he seen the mouth of a really great river.

He had wanted to stay near land and carry on his explorations, but his eyes troubled him so much that he went to bed and to sleep. He was locked in his cabin when his flagship went by the great pearl fisheries behind Margarita.

But the knowledge grew, as he failed to find a passage, that he had, indeed, discovered a continent.

I believe this is a very great continent which until today has been unknown. And reason aids me greatly because of that so great river and fresh water sea, and next the saying of Edras in his 4th book, chapter 6, which says that the six parts of the world are of dry land and one of water.... And this be a continent it is a marvelous thing, and will be among all the wise, since so great a river flows that it makes a fresh water sea of 48 leagues.

According to an old adage, "A little knowledge is a dangerous thing." That was surely true with Columbus. He put together the Bible, the writings of scientists of his own and an earlier time, and his own experience and came up with answers. All of them were wrong. He knew that he had found "an Other world" but he still thought that he was near Asia. Why weren't the natives black, since they lived on the latitude of Africa? Or brown since they were close to Asia? These questions bothered Columbus, but they didn't shape his thinking.

Having decided that this was a new continent he wanted to explore it, and if he had, the rest of his life would have been different and America would probably have been named Columbia; but his duty was to return to Hispaniola. On his way he passed the beautiful island that he named Margarita for the bride of Don Juan.

As they sailed Columbus pieced his bits of knowledge together and decided that he had skirted the Garden of Eden "where the sun rose on Creation." There was the fruit, the gold, and the river that went "out of Eden to water the garden; and from thence it was parted, and became four" (Genesis 2:10).

He also decided that the world wasn't round; it was the shape of a pear. The small end of the pear reached nearer heaven and on it the Terrestrial Paradise was located. This conclusion wasn't all fancy. He drew it from his inaccurate observations of Polaris. The idea that he had skirted the Garden of Eden seemed completely accurate to him—so accurate that he shared the conclusion with his royal sovereigns.

On August 15 Columbus left Margarita for Hispaniola. On August 20 he sighted it, and on August 31 he anchored in the port of Santo Domingo.

For a long time he had been troubled with worries about Hispaniola. What was Bartholomew doing? Were things going smoothly in Santo Domingo? What was the attitude of the Indians?

At Santo Domingo he was met by his brother, Diego. It was good to see him, but it was bad to hear all the news he had to tell.

Bartholomew had built the fort at Santo Domingo as Columbus had ordered. Gold had been discovered when the stone for the town was quarried, and for a time the Spaniards were happy. Then came ship-loads of supplies from Spain. Again everybody was happy. Bartholomew had paid a state visit to the cacique, Behechia, and had been royally received.

But the good things ended. Before Columbus had left for Spain he had named Francisco Roldan to be chief justice of the island. When Roldan heard the grievances against the Columbus brothers he organized all the malcontents into a revolt. A battle went on between Roldan, who wanted Bartholomew's position, and Bartholomew. When a message came from the royal sovereigns naming Bartholomew as adelantado, Roldan retreated to the court of the cacique, Behechia. Bartholomew followed Roldan, burning villages belonging to tribes that supported his opponent, but he didn't capture the man.

When Diego told Columbus of Roldan's treachery,

of the illness of the Spaniards—30 percent of them had syphilis—and that three caravels loaded with supplies which Columbus had sent from the Canaries had never arrived in Santo Domingo, the Admiral was dismayed. When he learned that the supply caravels had been induced to give their cargoes to Roldan and most of the criminals who were on board had joined the outlaws to attack Santo Domingo, he knew he had to take desperate measures.

October 18, 1499, Columbus sent two ships back to Spain loaded with brazil wood and slaves. Did not the Spaniards enslave the people of the Canary Islands? Did not Portugal enslave the negroes of Africa? No doubt the slaves would come in contact with Christianity. Poor Fray Ramón Pane had built just one chapel and baptized very few Indians, and he couldn't make any headway against the sinful Spaniards. In his letter Columbus asked for more good priests, for an educated man to administer justice, and for men and ships to defeat Roldan. He also suggested that rebellious settlers should be sent back to Spain and replaced with good, honest colonists.

Perhaps he didn't realize how his letter would sound to Ferdinand and Isabella. The Garden of Eden which he now wished to colonize? The pear-shaped world? Plenty of poetic descriptions of scenery but no practical facts. The royal sovereigns would know from his letters that Columbus was a sick man.

And he was sick. In fact he became so ill that he feared an actual encounter with Roldan whose men, counting the criminals from the Spanish ships, now outnumbered his. Instead of facing him he made a humiliating agreement which restored Roldan to office, erased all accusations against him, and gave land grants to the rebels who wanted to remain in the new world.

Columbus didn't know, of course, what was going on in Spain. Hojeda, hearing news of pearls in Paria, got permission from Fonseca to go to Paria. With him went Bartolome Roldan from the third voyage, Juan de la Cosa from the second, and a man who had had no part in the explorations, Amerigo Vespucci. Amerigo predated the account of his travels and gave the impression that he was first in the new land—thus, America. Hojeda discovered the pearl fisheries that Columbus had missed, named the area Venezuela (Little Venice), then sailed to Hispaniola. Another man who had sailed with Columbus, Peralones Niño, obtained a license for a voyage and returned to Spain with bushels of pearls. Vincente Yáñez Pinzón discovered the mouth of the Amazon.

How unsuccessful the three Columbus brothers had been! While they had given Spain a whole new world and opened for Christianity the opportunity for undreamed-of growth, as viceroy and adelantado they were weak when they should have been strong, firm when they should have been benign, foolish when they should have been wise.

Clearly the royal sovereigns should accede to Columbus's request for an educated and experienced man to administer justice. They chose Francisco de Bobadilla.

CHAPTER SIXTEEN

Francisco de Bobadilla seemed to the royal sovereigns just the man that Columbus had requested to administer justice. He was an old friend of the crown, knight of one of the orders of chivalry, and seemingly a man of good judgment. They gave him the power to arrest rebels, to take over forts, and to require obedience in all things from the Columbus brothers.

Bobadilla had heard that these brothers were the "vilest of men, evil enemies and shedders of Spanish blood" who were not only evil, according to malcontents, but took pleasure in the terrible things they did. They were wild beasts, "and what was worse they were the king's enemies."

He probably took much of this to be malicious gossip, but when his ship entered the harbor of Santo Domingo the first thing he saw was a gallows. Seven Spaniards were hanging there, and he soon learned that five more would be hanged the next day. Certainly what he had heard in Spain was true. He put Diego, the only brother in Santa Domingo at the moment, in chains. When Columbus came back he also was put in chains. Bartholomew was free, but Columbus—believing in the justice of Ferdinand and Isabella—advised him to give himself up without resistance. He, too, was put in chains.

Evidently the royal sovereigns didn't know Bobadilla as they thought they did. He took testimony only from the malcontents, held a trial of sorts, and sentenced the three brothers to return to Spain in chains. When they were put on board ship he held Columbus's house, all his papers, all his possessions. The admiral was returning to Spain without any of the gold that was really his.

The moment Columbus was packed on board the caravel, *La Guardia*, the captain begged to relieve him of the neck irons and heavy foot fetters he had worn from the time of his arrest through the hazardous journey. Wracked with arthritis Columbus could scarcely support them, but he said they had been placed there by authority of the royal sovereigns and only by that authority would he have them removed.

Columbus knew that no one in all of Spain would understand the problems of handling gold-grabbing Spaniards and a whole population different in language and customs and life style from any group in Europe. He knew that, in spite of his mistakes, he had made Spain the richest of countries. He ended a letter to a friend with, "God our Lord is present with His strength and wisdom, as of old, and in the end especially punisheth ingratitude and injuries."

In October Columbus landed in Cadiz and, still in chains and accompanied by a guard, went to stay at a monastery in Seville. Here he wrote:

It is now seventeen years since I came to serve these princes with the Enterprise of the Indies; they made me pass eight of them in discussion, and at the end rejected it as a thing of jest. None the less I persisted therein....

Over there I have placed under their sovereignty more land than there is in Africa and Europe and more than seventeen hundred islands....In seven years I, by divine will, made the conquest. At a time when I was entitled to expect rewards and retirement, I was incontinently arrested and with slight service to their highnesses.

The accusation was brought out of malice, on the basis of charges made by civilians who had revolted and wished to take possession of the lands. And he who did it had the order to remain as governor....By whom and where would this be considered just? I have lost in this enterprise my youth, my proper share in these things, and my honor....

I beg your graces, with the zeal of faithful Christians in whom their Highnesses have confidence, to read all my papers, and to consider how I who came from so far to serve these princes...now at the end of my days has been despoiled of my honor and my property without cause, wherein is neither justice nor mercy.

But it was six weeks before the royal sovereigns ordered him released from his chains and invited the three brothers to Granada. They sent Columbus two thousand ducats since Bobadilla had not allowed him to bring even an ounce of gold with him and he had been living on charity.

On December 17, 1500, Columbus and his two brothers appeared before the royal sovereigns in the Alhambra at Granada. Kissing the hands of Ferdinand and Isabella, Columbus couldn't control the tears that ran down his cheeks. Isabella wept, too, and she and the king tried to comfort their admiral. They demanded that he be given the income and rights that Bobadilla had taken from him. They would send a special agent to look after his interests. They said they knew how great the service was that he had given them.

Columbus listened for the one thing that he wanted most to hear. He wanted Bobadilla brought back to Spain and punished, and he wanted once again to be Viceroy of all the Indies.

For months he waited. It was some comfort that the royal sovereigns were gracious but most disturbing that they had other things on their minds. It was good to have his brothers, Bartholomew and Diego, with him. It was even better to have his twenty-year-old son Diego and his twelve-year-old son Ferdinand close by, but he still longed to get out to sea again.

Fray Gaspar Gorricio who had been his host while he waited at Seville now became his scribe. He made copies of Columbus's *Journals* written on his second and third voyages and four copies of his *Book of Privileges*. But the most important book he copied was the *Book of Prophecies*. Columbus knew the Bible well. From it he had copied all the prophecies that he felt were fulfilled by his voyages of discovery. Certainly he felt that he was "a man of destiny" long before his first voyage. It was this faith that kept him patient through the years of trying to interest someone in the voyage, that helped him withstand unaccountable trials on the ocean and on the land, always with the thought that prophecy must be fulfilled. To the Bible prophecies he added prophetic statements like those from Seneca:

An age will come after many years when the Ocean will loose

the chains of things, and a huge land be revealed, when Typhys will disclose new worth and Thule no more be the ultimate.—Medea

Some students believe that this book was written for the eyes of the queen who had a mystical and religious nature. But to one who studies Columbus's victory over disappointment and defeat, it seems the real core of his life.

While a half dozen representatives of Spain and Portugal were exploring America, Columbus, who had made it all possible, was waiting, waiting, waiting.

On September 3, 1501, Don Nicoles de Ovando was appointed governor and supreme justice of the "Island and Mainland of the Indies" except for parts to be governed by Yáñez Pinzón and Alonso de Hojeda. Columbus had waited for justice that would never come. Ovando sailed February 13, 1502, with an armada of thirty vessels!

But Columbus kept trying. He thought he could find a westward passage on the west side of Cuba. He would sail through this strait to India and come home to Spain from the East.

On March 4, 1502, the royal sovereigns authorized a fourth voyage for their Admiral of the Ocean Seas.

CHAPTER SEVENTEEN

It was 1502 and Columbus was fifty-one. His hair was completely white, and he suffered so much from arthritis that it was painful for him to move. Yet he started off on "the high voyage" with every intention of making it the best of his lifetime.

He didn't have the ships he had specially designed for exploration. He would have to make do with ships that could be chartered. But he was happy. His son, Diego, was at court; Beatriz Harana was taken care of; and young Ferdinand, now thirteen, as well as his brother Bartholomew would sail with him. True, he was no longer governor of Hispaniola. He couldn't even call there on his way to his new explorations, but when the trip was finished he felt that his privileges would be restored to him. Everything depended on this voyage.

There were four caravels in his fleet and one hundred and forty men and boys (all but five of them were receiving pay). While more than half were boys under sixteen, there were many who had voyaged with Columbus before and proved their strength and loyalty.

The fleet set sail "in the name of the Trinity"

May 9, 1502. Before leaving for the New World on May 25 it made a trip to Martinique. Although Columbus had been ordered not to put in at Santo Domingo he decided to disobey that order. One of his caravels, the *Santiago*, was not good f r the exploration he had planned. He would trade er for a faster ship at Santo Domingo. Besides a hurricane was building, and his fleet needed shelter He had ridden out one hurricane and was not eager to encounter another.

He put down anchor and sent a polite note to Ovando, the new governor of Hispaniola, asking permission to come ashore. He also warned Ovando of the building storm and advised him to keep the Spanish armada in the Santo Domingo harbor.

Ovando refused the request and mocked at the warning. "Is Columbus a prophet and a soothsayer?" he asked his friends. He sent the thirty ships to sea.

Abruptly the hurricane struck. Some ships sank; some were driven on the rocks and beaten to bits. Bobadilla, who had put Columbus and his brothers in chains, was on one of the vessels that went down. Also drowned were Antonio de Torres, Columbus's friend, and his most loyal Indian supporter, the cacique Guacanagari. Down, too, went the large shipment of gold that was meant for the royal sovereigns, including a great nugget. Nearly all of the thirty ships were lost; four struggled back to Santo Domingo. Only one of the thirty made it to Spain. This was the one carrying the gold that belonged to Columbus; it was delivered to his son, Diego. The whole city of Santo Domingo was laid flat.

What kind of awful power did Columbus have to cause such a hurricane, his enemies asked.

Columbus had anchored his fleet west of Santo Domingo in the mouth of a small river. It didn't escape the hurricane entirely but managed to ride out the storm.

Columbus had originally intended to begin his explorations at Margarita and follow the shoreline until he came to a strait. But when he decided to trade the *Santiago* at Santo Domingo he had had to make other plans. When he left the small shelter of the river's mouth he headed straight westward into unknown waters.

Now he saw evidences of a higher civilization among the Indians. There were bigger dugout canoes, some carrying as many as twenty men as well as their women and children. Instead of skeins of cotton they offered sleeveless shirts, shawls, copper tools, and other manufactured articles for trade. These weren't simple folks like the Arawaks. The women even covered their faces like Moslems. Columbus was now off the coast of Honduras.

The natives urged him to stop and explore the interior. Had he done so he would have found plenty of gold. But he was a single-minded man. He was intent on finding a strait that would lead him to the Indies.

Along the coast of Honduras his fleet encountered terrible weather for twenty-eight days—rain, thunder, lightning, and violent head winds. The crew was so frightened that the men made vows to go on pilgrimages if they were allowed to live through this nightmare.

In the midst of all this despair there was one bright

spot for Columbus. Ferdinand was proving himself a man. When the storm was over, the fleet coasted southward along the eastern shore of Nicaragua. It was here that Columbus learned from the natives that he was on an isthmus. There was no strait. He had been so sure that he could find a strait and make this last voyage his best. He had neither the men nor the provisions for a land exploration of the isthmus. Furthermore he was not interested. If there were no strait to discover, he must find something of value to take back to Spain. The royal sovereigns must not write off the fourth voyage as a total failure. Gold. . . he must find gold.

And find gold he did at Veragua. The natives were unfriendly so Columbus took only samples, deciding that more gold could be found on a later journey. But when he came to the end of the gold country he couldn't go back to his rich find. There were winds that carried him to the harbor of Puerto Bella.

He left Puerto Bella, but was driven back by the storms. The crew lived through another terrible twenty-eight days. This time the seamen didn't vow to go on pilgrimages if they were allowed to live. Instead they longed to die to "end this dreadful suffering." Besides being weary and wet, they were hungry. Ferdinand wrote:

What with the heat and dampness, our ship biscuit had become so wormy that, God help me, I saw many who waited for darkness to eat the porridge made of it, that they might not see the maggots; and others were so used to eating them that they didn't even trouble to pick them out, because they might lose their supper had they been so nice.

It was Christmas 1503 and the storms still battered the little armada trying to return to Veragua to look for more gold. Christmas was celebrated on the ships.

Had Columbus had the spirit and inspiration that had moved him on earlier voyages he might have sent his boats up the Chagres River within ten miles of the Pacific Ocean. The men might have made it to the Western Sea on foot and have been the first Europeans to see the Pacific. But something had gone out of Columbus!

At the mouth of the Rio Belen the Spaniards found the Indians specially friendly. Columbus met with the cacique who gave the party permission to explore the river. Columbus felt so secure that he brought his caravels in over the bar when the tide came in and started to build a fort. Sixty men explored the Rio Veragua and found a place where gold could be mined with ordinary knives. This was fabulous country!

Exploration continued in spite of rain. Suddenly the rain stopped; the water level sank until there was only two feet over the bar. The ships were locked in. The Spaniards had been sneaking out in twos and threes to rob the Indians. Now was the time for the Indians to get even. They began by visiting the ships in their warlike array. One of Columbus's best friends, Diego Montez, volunteered to find out what was going on. A mile or two away from Columbus's headquarters he saw an encampment of a thousand Indians. He stepped on shore, alone, to speak with them, then kept them in sight all night. In the morning he reported to Columbus.

Columbus said he needed more information. Diego Montez, with one companion, visited the encampment. He pretended that he had come to dress an arrow wound for the chief. He got into the "palace." Here he took out a barber kit—a comb, scissors, and mirror—and sat on the ground while his companion cut his hair. The cacique was so interested that he had a haircut, too, and then Diego Mendez gave him the kit. They all ate happily together and Mendez, who had learned the language readily, found out all he wanted to know.

"The only safe thing for us to do," he told Columbus, "is to take the chief and hold him ransom until we can get our ships out."

Columbus's brother, Bartholomew, undertook the task. He did seize the chief man and his household, but the cacique escaped.

Suspense was high until the water rose enough to liberate two of the ships. All of the company except twenty men and a wolfhound that were left at the newly built fort were working on the caravels. Four hundred Indians appeared suddenly at the fort armed with bows and arrows, spears and slingshots. The battle lasted three hours. Finally the Indians withdrew. One Spaniard was killed and several others, including Bartholomew Columbus, were wounded.

Another party that had gone up the river to get a supply of water was killed by the Indians.

Columbus would have left the Rio Belen immediately, but one of his ships, the *Gallega*, was still behind the bar and Bartholomew was lying wounded in the fort.

While the battle was going on, Columbus lay ill on

the *Capitana*, a mile offshore. He was delirious with malarial fever. He heard the voices of the fighting men followed by silence. Of it he wrote:

I climbed to the highest part of the ship, and in a fearful voice cried out for help to Your Highnesses' war captains in every direction; but none replied. At length, groaning from exhaustion, I fell asleep and heard a compassionate voice saying: "O fool and slow to believe and serve thy God, the God of every man! What more did He do for Moses, or for David, His servant, than for thee? From thy birth He ever held thee in special charge. When He saw thee arrive at man's estate, marvelously did He cause thy name to resound over the earth. The Indies, so rich a portion of the world, he gave thee for thine own, and thou hast divided them as it pleased thee. Of those barriers of the Ocean Sea, which were closed with such mighty chains, he gave thee the keys. What more did He do for the people of Israel, for David who from a shepherd He raised to be king over Judea? Turn to him and acknowledge thy fault; thine old age shall not hinder thee from mighty deeds, for many and vast heritages he holdeth....Fear not, but have trust; all these tribulations are written on tablets of marble, and not without cause." I heard all this in a swoon, but I had no answer to give in definite words, only to weep for my transgressions.

The Indians retired, but there were no hostages to secure the safety of Bartholomew, the other men in the fort, and the *Gallega*. Pedro de Ledesma, more courageous and a better swimmer than most, swam across the bar. He brought back the news that the men were quarreling with each other, their supplies were low, and they wanted to come on board.

Columbus gave up Santa Maria de Belen where gold could be mined so readily. Diego Mendez brought the men over the bar in dugout canoes, and the *Gallega* was left to rot in the harbor.

CHAPTER EIGHTEEN

Columbus and his tiny fleet had battled storms and heavy seas. They had endured more than most men and ships. Ten members of the crew had been lost in the Battle of Belen. But a hidden enemy was at work. Worms were making the wooden ships into sieves.

Now Columbus knew that he would have to give up his dream of making the fourth voyage his greatest success. He planned to go to Santo Domingo to repair his ships and rest his men, and then go back, defeated, to Spain. The trouble was that the pilots and captains thought Columbus didn't know what he was doing. They had come for gold, and they intended to find it.

To avoid mutiny, Columbus gave up his plan and adopted theirs.

At Porto Bello he had to abandon *Vizcaino* and go on with only *Capitana* and *Santiago*. In these two ships the men pumped night and day, and every pan and kettle was used to bail out water. Two leaking ships, few provisions, weary men, a sick admiral, and the wind, current, and sea were all against them

On June 23 Columbus gave up, grounded the two vessels, and built the ships into a sort of fort. These ships would never sail again. And what about the men? The provisions were all gone except sea biscuit, oil, and vinegar. The men thought that they could replenish their supplies from the Indians, but wherever that had been done the Indians had become warlike. The men were ordered to stay in the fort.

Mendez and his two companions went alone into the interior. He had a way with the Indians and arranged for them to bring food to the Spaniards in return for trading truck. The Spaniards wouldn't starve, but how would they ever get home?

In July Diego Mendez offered to go by Indian canoe to Hispaniola to ask for a rescue ship. Taking one Christian and six Indians with him he left in the converted canoe. Once he was surrounded by cannibal Indians and had to turn back. But again he tried, this time with a companion canoe. Each canoe carried seven Christians and ten Indians.

Finally, after incredible suffering, the canoes reached Xaraqua where Ovando was fighting Indians. Mendez went on foot to his headquarters. Ovando kept Mendez with him at Xaraqua for seven months—from August 1503 until March 1504, when he was allowed to leave for Santo Domingo.

In Santo Domingo there was a seaworthy caravel that could have been used to save Columbus and his men, but Ovando refused to send it out. Mendez would have to wait until other ships arrived from Spain.

Columbus, Bartholomew, and young Ferdinand, waiting almost without hope with the other men at

Santa Gloria—the fort contrived from the two caravels—were not having an easy time. Spaniards, forbidden to leave the fort, were ready for mutiny. When men are ready to revolt, leaders arise, Columbus knew. The Porras brothers were the leaders. They had convinced themselves that Columbus had missed Santo Domingo on purpose.

Forty-eight men and boys who had joined the conspiracy piled into ten dugout canoes. They followed the coast, robbing the Indians every time they touched land. At first the sea was smooth, but when the winds grew strong they decided to put back. This they couldn't do, either. They threw everything they owned overboard. Next they threw over the Indians they had taken along to paddle the canoes and when the Indians panicked and hung to the gunwales they cut off their hands. Finally they had to start back to Santa Gloria by land, on foot, stealing from the Indians as they went along.

Meanwhile Columbus and his fifty loyal men did all right until the supply of food from the Indians became less and less and the Spaniards were again faced with starvation.

Columbus had an almanac which predicted eclipses. On February 29, 1504, there would be an eclipse. He summoned the caciques and chief men to a conference. Through an interpreter he gave a speech. Christians believed that God would reward the good and punish the wicked. See what had happened to the Porras brothers and the mutineers? God wasn't pleased with the Indians, either. Soon he would show them just how displeased he was. Columbus told them to watch that night and see what happened.

The Indians watched. The eclipse began just as the moon rose. As the eclipse progressed the Indians came running to the fort with provisions. They begged Columbus to call off the eclipse. "I must pray," he said and retired to his cabin. He may have prayed but he certainly did something else too. The eclipse gave him the opportunity to compute the longitude of Jamaica.

Now there was food, but each day there was less hope of rescue. Another mutiny was building when a small caravel sent by Ovando appeared. Mendez sent a message that he had reached Santo Domingo and would send a rescue ship as soon as a caravel was available.

Columbus now offered a general pardon to all the mutineers so that things would be in good order when the rescue ship came. The mutineers chose to fight rather than to come to terms. The mutineers lost and their leader, Francisco de Porras, was put in chains.

At the end of June 1504 the rescue caravel arrived at Santa Gloria. All of the Christians—about one hundred—went on board. The long wait—more than a year—was over. Columbus's most desperate prayers were answered.

The trip to Santo Domingo took six and a half weeks. When the ship anchored and the rescued men landed Ovando said that he was glad to see them. But he set Francisco de Porras free without punishment for the mutiny or the mutineers' treatment of the Indians.

September 12, 1504, Columbus, his brother Bartholomew, young Ferdinand, and twenty-two others set sail for Spain. The rest of the men decided to give up the ocean for a time. Some became the first settlers of Puerto Rico. Perhaps the decision to stay was a wise one. There was a broken mainmast, a sprung foremast, storms, and heavy seas on the way back to Spain, and the seamen were penniless. It was November 7, 1504, when their ship arrived safely at Sanlucar de Barrameda. Ferdinand was now sixteen, a man in strength and experience. Bartholomew was strong and ready for another adventure. Columbus at fifty-three was finished in body, mind, and spirit, though not yet willing to admit it.

He stopped at a pleasant house in Seville. Although he hadn't yet been paid for the money he had spent to charter the rescue ship and bring his seamen home, he was a wealthy man. The seamen, who had been paid six months in advance before the voyage began, had been gone from Spain thirty-two months. Those who couldn't pick up odd jobs depended upon their admiral for money to keep them alive.

Diego, who as a little boy had hung trustingly to his father's finger at the Convent of Rábida, had graduated from page boy to a member of the queen's bodyguard. King Ferdinand liked this handsome, blond young man of twenty-four, but he didn't intend to listen to his pleas for his father's cause. Columbus couldn't believe that Diego wouldn't be heard. He wrote:

Certain it is that I have served Their Highnesses with as great diligence and love as I might have employed to win paradise and more; and if in somewhat I have been wanting, that was impossible or much beyond my knowledge and strength. Our Lord God in such cases asketh no more of men than good will. . . .

Thy father who loveth thee more than himself.

The queen who had always been Columbus's friend at court, who had wept with him and consoled him, was on her deathbed. How pleased Columbus would have been to have kissed her hand and given her some of the golden trinkets he had brought from Veragua. But what if he had confronted his dying queen with miserable tales of how Ovando had mistreated him? No, the king and his confidants decided, it would be wiser not to invite him at all.

When the queen died Columbus was too ill to go to her funeral. Her bodyguard was dissolved, and Diego was invited to membership in the king's guard and given the title of Don.

Columbus was now sure that Diego could reach the king's ear. He wrote Diego letter after letter until even Diego must have grown tired of the often repeated story. When Diego could get no satisfaction from the king, Columbus sent his brother Bartholomew and his sixteen-year-old son Ferdinand to court.

At last he decided that he must speak for himself. He wanted the title of Admiral of the Ocean Seas to be hereditary in his family. He also wanted to be Viceroy of the Indies, and he wanted the share of the riches from the New World that he felt belonged to him. He tried to arrange to cross Spain in a fancy hearse that had been built for the funeral of a high church official. He gave this up and sought permission

113

from the king to ride a mule. (The horse interests in Spain had outlawed mule riding, but Columbus thought a horse's livelier gait would be too much for his arthritis.) The king granted this humble request. He also granted an audience which netted Columbus nothing, since Columbus wouldn't compromise. He wanted all or nothing. Nothing was what he got.

Finally Columbus realized that he would never again be Governor of Hispaniola. He was too sick to stand the sea voyage. Now he asked that Diego inherit the title Admiral of the Ocean Seas. To this the king consented. He also asked that Diego be made governor of Hispaniola. The king thought that Diego was too young for such a responsibility. (Six years later Diego was made governor of Hispaniola for a time.)

In May 1506 Columbus made his last will and testament. He made some small bequests to pay debts of honor. He set aside a sum toward a crusade to regain the Holy Land from the Turks. But the bulk of his property and all of his privileges he left to his son, Diego, who was to be responsible for the welfare of his uncles, his brother Ferdinand, and Beatriz de Harana.

Columbus was dying. His sons, Diego and Ferdinand, his younger brother Diego (Bartholomew was at court), his most loyal friend, Diego Mendez, and a few other faithful friends and servants gathered at his bedside. A priest came, a mass was read, and everybody received the sacrament. The priest performed the last rites and Columbus said, "Father, into thy hands I commend my spirit."

Columbus never realized how many prophecies he

had fulfilled. With little glory the man died who had "felt himself to be in the hand of God" as he opened a whole new world to Christianity.